I0408038

LEADERSHIP FOR A LIFETIME

TONY MORRIS

TABLE OF CONTENTS

DEDICATION

This book is dedicated to the memory of my friend and brother James L. Giles

ACKNOWLEDGEMENTS

I am not sure that any of us can fully appreciate the paths of all of those that we have crossed who have positively influenced us. However, there are those who leave an indelible impression on our souls and some of those are whom I wish to acknowledge. My journey as a leader has been and still is amazing and I greatly appreciate the people who have positively impacted my life.

Some of those that have impacted or greatly influenced my life as a leader have not always done so directly. There are those that have done so indirectly whether it is through their writings or speaking.

I acknowledge the leadership of my wife and partner, Renee. Your commitment to assisting people in the development of understanding their purpose in life and their gifts is admirable.

To my mother, who is the first human leader that I had in my life. Your example of doing what it took for us to make it is appreciated.

To the sports coaches that I remember as examples and father figures in my life. You were the men that pushed me, encouraged me, challenged me and brought out the best in me. Thank you, to Mr. Williams (baseball), Lamar Mills (football), Mike Yasutake and John Yasutake (football), Walt Atkinson (basketball), and Al Hairston (basketball).

To the men and women that are or have been friends, mentors, peer mentors and indirect mentors in my life. Your leadership examples have been a source of inspiration to me:

Bishop Eugene and Mother Coreather Drayton	Bishop Wiley Jackson
Pastor Larry Brooks	Bishop Stanley and Co-Pastor Dee Williams
Bishop Carlton Pearson	Bishop David and Dr. Claudette Copeland

Archbishop E. Bernard and Pastor Debra Jordan

Prophet James L. Giles

Dr. Myles and Ruth Munroe

Bishop Joshua Turnel and Pastor Jocelyn Nelson

Apostle Jefferson Edwards

Apostle Clifford Turner

Pastors Casey and Wendy Treat

Pastor Ray Frederick

Apostle Fred and Betty Price

Bishop Earl Paulk

Reverend Dennis Peacocke

Pastor A.R. Bernard

Pastor Mensa Otabil

Bob Harrison

Apostle Bertril Baird

Gregg Alex

Rocco Errico

Dr. Sam Chand

Bishop George Archie

Evangelist Amanda Irving

Professor Hitendra Wadhwa

If there is anyone that may feel left off of this list of acknowledgements and believes that they should be a part of it, please know that it is not intentional.

Introduction

Is this just another book about leadership? If you check, you will find that there seems to be thousands of books on leadership that approach the subject from every possible, angle. So why would I want to write another one? That is a great question! I wanted to write this book because leaders, leadership training and leadership development have been a curiosity and a passion of mine for more than thirty-five years. I have seen leaders come and I have seen leaders go. I have observed and worked with what would be considered great leaders and I have observed and worked with what would be considered ineffective leaders. I have found that true leaders are the **engine** behind, underneath and to human ingenuity. In my experience, very few individuals, people and projects reach their maximum potential without some form of leadership being exercised. There are leaders in various domains of life from the home to a business to an organization to a community to a nation. There are leaders in areas ranging from human rights to social justice to small business development to science to entertainment to sports to physics and so many others.

Leaders and leadership are not monolithic subjects. However, the terms are full of meaning; if you and I were to ask ten different people to explain to us what a leader is and what leadership is, we might get ten different answers. Therefore, I believe that we must be cautious about approaching a discussion about leaders and leadership as though we (all) think and see them the same. The subjects of leaders and leadership can be as broad or exhaustive, as diverse or conversely, as narrow as we choose to make them. This is because leaders and leadership give context or a frame of reference through a person or a group of people because of their efforts, their inspiration, their influence and their examples to the human experience. As important true leaders reveal, expose and demonstrate what is possible for the future of people.

Generally speaking, a leader is someone who at one point or another in their life was probably a follower. How did they become a leader? Was it, as some suggest, a birthright or are there other factors that we may need to consider to find out what makes a leader a leader? Do people in general have the capability to become a leader or is there a certain criterion that must be met first?

One thing that is for certain is that it is sometimes difficult to define what a leader and leadership really is. Yet, there are those occasions when we see someone in action and we recognize without a doubt that we are observing a leader. Could this be because maybe there is no single definition for what a leader is and that quite possibly leadership is really an essence from which flows a function? Could it be that leadership is an identity that someone assumes at a given time in their lives?

There have been several scientific studies done around what leadership is, and unfortunately many of those studies convolute the subject further. For instance, one leadership theory suggests that to be a leader someone must emerge from an elite group of people. Another theory offers that leaders are born that way and not made or developed to be leaders. Finally, one other theory suggests that leadership is a role that someone plays much like an actor portraying a part in a film or a play. For me what is bothersome about these theories is that there may be hints of reality in these ideas however, the real question is do these theories fully or clearly explain what a leader or leadership is? I would suggest that these theories and others similar to them are actually extremely limiting and place limitations on what is possible for individuals and groups when it comes to the matriculation of potential leaders.

I see leaders and leadership similar to a person who peers through a window in a house and looks beyond what is inside of the house that they are standing in. In some way, they may be peering into the future of what is possible beyond their own or others current or previous experiences. However, let's just say that looking through the window to what is outside is not fulfilling to them. They want to step outside of the house because they have seen something that they believe can be beneficial not only to themselves, but to all of those in the house and all of those who may at one-time in the future enter into that house. In that instance, they don't generally ask questions like, what type of family did I come from or is this a role that I really want to play? No, they are driven by something deep down inside of themselves that says to them, you can, you will and you must. Sometimes the motivation driving them is a deep sense of confusion about what they are or have experienced. It can also be a dissatisfaction with observing injustices or mistreatment. Or, it could be that they recognize that there is much more than what is or has been experienced for themselves and others and they want to lead into a created future.

I may be describing you and your current existence, or you may be a seasoned veteran in the area of leadership and you simply want to continue the developmental process of discovering more effective and efficient ways of leading. Whatever the case may be, I want us to go together on this journey of developing our **Leadership For A Lifetime**. This will not be business as usual or maybe I should say it will not be 'leadership as usual.' We may be challenged to re-examine some of the fundamental ideas and beliefs that we have about leaders and leadership so that we can lead into the future on a more illuminated pathway.

In some instances, I will use scriptures from the Bible as a form of scientific explanation for universal leadership principles. My usage of scriptures as a science should not frighten traditional Christians because science is simply defined as an, "exact knowledge, truth ascertained, systematically arranged and showing the operation of general (or in our case, universal) laws." (Webster) In general, the term science has not been consistently applied to spirituality or western Christianity, but with a broader understanding of science we are learning that the scriptures are a body of scientific laws revealed from the eternal God. The scriptures are based upon an absolute set of unchanging principles of universal laws that can be proven under every circumstance and by which we as people can learn to solve the problems of life and produce the correct harmonious results intended for our lives.

It is out from this context we will discuss this idea of **Leadership For A Lifetime.**

PART ONE

PERSONAL LEADERSHIP

CHAPTER ONE

Authenticity

"The privilege of a lifetime is to become who you truly are."

C.G. Jung

Your leadership calling is not grounded in what anyone else is or has been. While other leaders may have had a positive influence in your life, your specific calling has to do with who you are at your core. It also has to do with who and what the Creator has imparted into you as your inherent nature. It has to do with you being an authentic person and learning to lead out from that place in your life. What does it mean to be or become an authentic person? The simplest definition that I can come up with for what it means to be authentic is "when your thoughts, words and behaviors are in alignment." Authenticity is given birth out of integrity or wholeness. When a person understands that they are or can be whole or fully themselves, that is when they are being or becoming authentic.

It is much more difficult to maintain a pretense than it is to be your real self. Learning to be yourself is the natural flow for our lives. However, if we have never discovered who we are or who we can truly be, then it is often challenging to identify the areas of our lives that we are thinking, talking and acting in a pretentious manner. It is also difficult being in complete harmony with our inner core when we come to believe that the pretense that we have maintained is the real us. Unfortunately, this is the way in which a number of people who are leaders see themselves. They have come to believe that they are a persona of some sort. I don't believe that very many people have consciously or intentionally said to themselves," I think I am going to be inauthentic today." Rather it is more probable that a person is more interested in being accepted, liked or significant to other people. Therefore, in their attempts to be acceptable or not look bad in the eyes of others, they don't function authentically in those relationships. They function at less or different than their true selves and therefore, are fundamentally living an inauthentic life. Anytime any of us chooses to avoid the challenges of life that may result in our being rejected, misunderstood or disliked over being true to what we know to be true for ourselves we are unable to function at our optimum capabilities. We are compromising who we as a person. Of course this cannot be good for us personally or anyone else connected to us.

I don't like thinking of myself as being inauthentic at any time or in anyway, yet I know that there have been numerous occasions that I have settled for or have been less than who I am at my core in a given situation. Whether it was the fear of being rejected or the attempt to become something different than I was created to be it wound up costing me in significant ways that I never could have measured. I was being inauthentic in those moments.

PERSONAL LEADERSHIP LESSON

I have personally known the effects of inauthenticity in my own life. In my formative years as a leader I was fixated on impressing others, making a name for myself and striving for what others deemed as success. It was many years later that I learned that the only way to authenticity is to let go of the external expectations of others and look internally to what you know is right for you to be and do.

Have you ever noticed yourself doing something similar? Today we live in a culture that if we are not careful will impose an expectation upon us through people, particularly if we are leaders or emerging leaders to look a certain way, fit into specific patterns or define success the way that it defines it. If we are not careful and more specifically if we are not living conscious lives, we can be shaped by a kind of subconscious cultural commitment in which we make a commitment to being something that we were never intended to be because of our own lack of self-worth or because of us succumbing to the expectations of others. This type of thinking and behavior causes us to become people pleasers or conformist to ideas that are not our own. Or ideas that we cannot fully commit ourselves to. The gravitational pull of these forces are not only psychological but they are also spiritual in nature. We can only overcome them when we are willing to acknowledge the ways in which we are thinking, talking and acting in an inauthentic manner. This thinking effects how we see and respond to situations and what the priorities are in our lives. "While we might think we are responding in true, authentic ways, what is actually happening is that our responses are essentially just a fallout of the conditions that we have submitted ourselves to. It is against that pull—the enormous gravitational force of that condition—that we attempt to be authentic." (1)

When we compromise who God has created us to be even in the smallest matters, it becomes easier for those compromises to become more and more acceptable in our lives. The way that the master teacher and trainer Jesus Christ explained it is, "Whoever can be trusted with very little can also be trusted with much, and whoever is dishonest with very little will also be dishonest with much" (Luke 16:10 NIV). It could probably be considered a little thing to truly be ourselves because who else are we supposed to be? It is much more of a task to be or become someone that we were never intended to be.

If we compromise our true selves to any degree, we may begin to live as if being that way is our norm. However, over time, this type of thinking and functioning erodes our sense of self and self-discovery. It reminds me of an illustration that I once heard about a person who was making a piece of pottery. The potter placed the lump of clay on the potter's wheel, and as she began spinning the wheel and shaping the piece of clay, she decided to put some red paint on the clay. She didn't put a lot of paint on the clay. It was just enough to alter the color of the clay slightly. When she first put the red paint on the clay, it was clearly noticeable; however, after she had spun the red paint into the clay on the potter's wheel you could barely tell that it was in there. The moral of the story is that if you didn't know what the clay looked like prior to the red paint being added, you may have thought that the way that it looked when she was finished making the piece of pottery from the clay was its original color. Most people who would see that piece of pottery after it was completed would have never thought to ask the question, "I wonder what color the clay was before she completed the piece of pottery." However, in life what we are often observing when we look at others or even ourselves is what we or they have become and not who they are originally created to be. The only one who knows our original or true potential for being is God the Creator and ultimately God unfolds us, to ourselves as the clay being shaped or even reshaped into what the Potter intended for us to be.

In addition, when the integrity and transparency of who we really are is conceded in some way, even when it is not easily detectable at first, our sense of ourselves gets obscured, making it harder to become our true selves. When that happens, our foundation as an authentic person is compromised and we may find ourselves either in conformity to others expectations or living below our God-given potential.

"To be authentic requires putting aspects of our present ways of being on the line—letting go of pretenses, *'letting God'* reveal things to us in new ways, and acknowledging whatever inauthenticity is in our lives." (**2** italics added) If we do this we will open the door to the possibility of our own potential. This can only take place in proportion to our being authentic. However, the only way for this to happen is that we must first acknowledge the degree to which we have been inauthentic in our lives. If we are unwilling to acknowledge the inauthenticity we are essentially resigning ourselves to the control of that inauthenticity. What we refuse to master may come back and master us. "Living with a pretense, or being afraid that some aspect of our lives might be discovered, precludes any real freedom." (**3**) According to the scriptures, freedom is rooted in truth. It says, "you shall know the truth and the truth will make you free" (John 8:32 KJV). Also if we are unwilling to acknowledge where we have been inauthentic, we may be living in a false sense of freedom. When you are not fully operating in the freedom that has been given to you by the Creator, the price of living as though you are free is too high to pay. Why pretend to be when we really are not? The amount of energy that goes into maintaining appearances has become a multi-billion-dollar industry. We and others are contributing to it every single day when we live out from its ideas.

Jean-Paul Sartre said, "that, facing one's freedom can be terrifying and uncomfortable—because facing it makes one feel insecure, and inevitably produces some level of anguish." To maintain any pretense, we have to persuade ourselves that our actions are determined— by some external force or source. It doesn't mean that external forces or sources cannot influence us however, the reality is that our actions are determined by our own internal choices. Often those choices are made even before we have a conscious thought about them. Our subconscious minds are often the drivers of these thoughts.

Harvard Professor Chris Argyris (1991) who after forty years of studying human behavior and tendencies on the subject of our inauthenticity says, "Put simply, people consistently act inconsistently, unaware of the contradiction between their espoused theory and their theory-in-use, between the way they think they are acting, and the way the really act." Therefore, the means by which we move into authenticity is by confronting the barriers to our being authentic.

I believe that we should begin this part of our discussion by asking what factors have gone into making you who you are. "What core beliefs do you fundamentally live by? What are your key motivators for your life? Which techniques do you primarily apply when operating in your leadership gifting? What practices do you consistently engage in as a way of life? What are the environments that have most influenced your thinking as a person?" (**4**)

Some people may operate from the belief that there are certain things about themselves that are permanent and cannot be changed. Some of those things are not changeable; their personality, their emotional traits, their intelligence and their character. There are a number of traditionally trained scientists that have been trained to believe that we are mostly locked into who we are or can become once we reach a certain age. They also believe we have <u>inherent</u> strengths and <u>inherent</u> weaknesses, which is the argument of some traditional geneticists. Others believe that we will not or possibly even cannot change many things once we reach adulthood, which is the argument of some traditional neuroscientists. The final argument comes from a broader group of people who believe that our objective in life should be to identify and leverage our strengths upon or over others," which is a form of believing that one group is or can somehow be superior to another person or group of people. (**5**)

The new science suggests something much different. It suggests that we can change if we choose to. However, we must ask some real questions. What aspect(s) of ourselves are we actually open to change? Which aspect(s) of ourselves are we not open to change? It comes down to what type of mindset we are operating from. If we are operating from a locked mindset that doesn't believe that change is possible then we will not invest the energy necessary into producing the changes that are possible for us. On the other hand, if we are operating from a mindset that embraces growth and development we can begin to move towards the authentic life that we desire to live and assist others in doing the same.

"People with a locked mindset are generally people who are:

1. More interested in performance as the ultimate goal.

2. Not very comfortable in stepping out of their comfort zone.

3. Often comparing themselves with people that they believe are inferior to them.

4. Easily discouraged by failure.

People with a growth and development mindset are generally people who:

1. Believe you can train yourself over time so that your first response to challenges is learning and not fear.

2. Recognize that you can further develop your talents and abilities.

3. Believe that "if you believe you can do it, or if you believe you cannot, in either case you are right."

To produce a growth and development mindset, we must be willing to step out of our comfort zones. A person who is not committed to growing beyond where they are will want to keep proving that they are good at something even though it is the same task that they have already gained mastery of again and again. They build their value around how good they have become at something and not what they can look for next to challenge themselves to grow. This type of thinking can become a barrier to any real growth and development. People that are committed to growth and development lose interest once they are doing well at something and they look to step out of their comfort zones." **(6)**

A leader must learn to push beyond the fear of criticism. It's a barrier that keeps a leader in a locked mindset. Such a leader loses interest when they are told about errors they have made and how these errors could be corrected. The opposite is true for the person with a growth and development mindset. These types of people continue to pay attention to feedback about their errors and how they can be corrected, even when it is uncomfortable.

Additionally, the barrier of dealing with failure becomes important to a person who is becoming authentic. Generally, failure is addressed one of two ways, "I failed so I must not be any good at this" or "I failed so I must increase my efforts and correct my approach to doing better or my best in this situation."

The last barrier to authenticity that I will mention is comparisons. I have run into more than my share of leaders who are interested in the failure of others. When they are extremely insecure, they often feel good about themselves because of the failure of someone else. This mindset produces nothing but inauthenticity because why would there be any comfort in the failure of someone else? This can only take place as a reflection of that person's understanding of themselves. More importantly we should be interested in learning from the successes and the failures of others as opposed to being critical of them.

Stephen R. Covey indicates that "when we are true to the light we have been given, when we keep our word consistently, when we are striving continually to harmonize our habit system with our value system, then our life is integrated or *(authentic)*." He goes on to say, "The internal security that emerges from it eliminates the need to live for impression, to exaggerate for effort, to drop names or places, to borrow strength from credentials or possessions or fashions or affiliations or associations or status symbols." (**7**)

"To become authentic leaders, we must discard the myth that leadership means having legions of supporters following us as we ascend to the pinnacles of power. Only then can we realize that authentic leadership is serving people by aligning them around a common mission and values and empowering them on their leadership journeys. This transformation from I to We is the most important process leaders go through in becoming authentic." (**8**)

CHAPTER ONE: REFLECTIONS

Your leadership calling is not grounded in what anyone else is or has been.

The simplest definition that I can come up with for what it means to be authentic is "when your thoughts, words and behaviors are in alignment."

"To be authentic requires putting aspects of our present ways of being on the line—letting go of pretenses, *'letting God'* reveal things to us in new ways, and acknowledging whatever inauthenticity is in our lives."

To produce a growth and development mindset we must be willing to step out of our comfort zones.

To become authentic leaders, we must discard the myth that leadership means having legions of supporters following us as we ascend to the pinnacles of power.

Leading from the Inside-Out

"Deep within, there is something profoundly known, not consciously, but subconsciously. A quiet truth, that is not a version of something, but an original knowing."

T.F. Hodge

"Personal Leadership is a state of mind and heart. It asks us to be fully present in our lives, awake to habitual behaviors and willing to look at every situation with fresh eyes. All real growth and progress is made step-by-step, following a natural sequence of development. We don't actually "become" leaders, as if leadership were an option among other choices. Rather as we emerge as our true selves we will then naturally be leaders. Every human has the instinct and capacity for leadership but most do not have the courage or will to cultivate it." **(1)**

"Very often our personal leadership potential is buried under cultural, social and ideological perceptions" that we allow to undermine our growth and development. If left unaddressed it can hinder our full emergence as a person. **(2)** This is why it is important to identify our inner core, access it and learn to live out from it. Many people have called the inner core the spirit or the soul. It is from this place that we must learn to lead…from the Inside-Out.

This process of learning to live from our inner core is a lifelong journey. However, we can become better and better at it as we put into practice some basic ideas that can enhance this process. We almost need to approach the understanding of our inner core like we would the discovery of a new invention. Often when someone has a new invention, they may have a basic idea of how that invention can work. However, in the initial stages, they may not recognize the new inventions fullest potential. Our lives are much the same in that we may have a basic idea of what our inner core is, but lack awareness of all we can be. This may be particularly true for those who have lived a little while longer than others. In my opinion, to say that you have mastered the understanding of your inner core without the need for additional exploration is be a mistake. Our lives are forever unfolding and we are capable of learning more about ourselves, even after living many decades in these bodies. We don't really know what types of treasures we may discover inside of ourselves unless we explore the inner core with the same passion and purpose with which we have explored some of the external aspects of our lives.

For millennia, people have attempted to understand what is really inside of themselves. Who are they at their core? What many come to realize is that there are spheres of awareness (consciousness) that can only be accessed from the inner core. Neville Goddard said, "it is only by a change of consciousness, by actually changing your concept of yourself, that you can 'build more stately mansions' – the manifestations of higher and higher concepts." As a matter of fact, it is only through the inner core that some of the most profound thoughts, ideas, impressions and intuitions have come into the lives of people. Unfortunately, many of the institutions of learning only draw from the external and reinforce their ideas through external stimuli as the primary motivation for understanding leadership. Therefore, when groups of leaders come together under that framework, they are not being trained to listen for or to look to better understand how they can lead from their inner core. Instead, they are listening for and wanting to learn the latest techniques or practices in leadership without recognizing that they are learning to lead from the outside-in and not the inside-out.

There are many thoughts or ideas that come to us through intuition and they may not be comprehensible to us in the moment. However, that doesn't mean that those same thoughts and ideas are not apprehensible by us. We have to learn to access those thoughts and ideas through practices that will allow us over time to comprehend what it is that we are apprehending. Some of those basic practices are prayer, meditation, study, and learning to live in simplicity. Many of the great leaders throughout history that many of us admire, respect or even follow their examples are women and men who engaged these simple practices.

How do we access our inner core? We access our inner core as our inner core! We must not see ourselves as separate and distinct from who we are internally. We are not bodies living in spirits rather we are spirits living in bodies. The spirit is the essence of who we are. The spirit knows what the mind has yet to understand. This may sound impractical to some; however, if we are intentional about learning to lead from the inside out, we must explore beyond human knowledge and learn to explore in human consciousness – spiritually. Human knowledge does not have to be counter-productive to human consciousness. The challenge we face when we only operate from a human knowledge paradigm is that we only know what we have learned. If we have not learned something, then we won't consciously know it. However, in human consciousness, we can intuitively know somethings that our minds have yet to fully comprehend. When we slow our lives down and eliminate unnecessary interferences, we become aware of things beyond our personal experiences. The Spirit of God then is able to disclose to us what has always been there awaiting our acknowledgment and acceptance. We have been given the capacity to be made aware of things beyond our personal experiences which is at the heart of faith. Yes, we will have to learn the proper application of these things, but this awareness that is beyond our experiences can become our actual experience. Many deep experiences in life are extremely difficult to explain, define or capture with words alone. For instance, how do you define or explain a parent's love for their child? How do you explain or capture the lengths to which a parent will go for the welfare of their child? It is often unfathomable intellectually; however, those of us that are parents can relate to what it is that we sense inside of ourselves when we hear someone talk about this subject. It is an awareness that has been given to each of us from God. It must be cultivated and nurtured to maturity.

What are some of the benefits of cultivating our inner core? Professor Hitendra Wadhwa of the Columbia University School of Business gives us some areas to focus on when it comes to developing our inner core. He informs us that through prayer and meditation we can:

1. Disconnect from the world around us and focus on one activity.

2. Still our bodies and focus on an inner activity.

3. Still our minds. Meditation is stillness of the mind.

4. Practice Mindfulness – "where is your mind" – Are you in the present moment?

He concluded that "wherever within your sphere of awareness your attention is directed – consciously or unconsciously – that is where your energy is." More than anything else, prayer and meditation help us to see ourselves as something more comprehensive than our bodies, emotions and even our thoughts.

To grow, we need to have an inner hunger for change. Sometimes this hunger rises naturally in us, like when someone's feedback or a setback makes us realize the need to develop a new strength or eliminate a weakness. At other times, we need to consciously kindle this hunger and keep it alive."

As we develop our inner core, some of the benefits that we will realize are:

1. It gives us tremendous strength, fortitude, resilience and courage in life.

2. It helps us to pull away from specific perceptions and feelings and create an open space of possibilities.

3. It trains us to command our minds to focus on anything that we choose. (**3**)

PERSONAL LEADERSHIP LESSON

Many times as leaders we believe that the busier that we are, the more effective we are. However, I have found that is not necessarily the case. Sometimes busyness is a distraction to long term productivity. Therefore, taking time to get centered has become a regular practice of mine. I have found that sometimes the busier I am, the less sensitive I have been to the needs of people that I am working with.

Some of the documented benefits of prayer and meditation are health and well-being – decreased stress and heightened stress resistance – better sleep or rest – lower blood pressure – stronger immune system – greater emotional tolerance – positive moods – reduced anxiety and reduced depression. It also provides stronger performance when we are working – improved concentration – faster and better learning – better memory – creative problem solving – stronger connections with other people – greater empathy and better impulse control.

"The motivation to become what God intended for us to become individually and collectively is done by an inner sculpting so that we can come closer to our ideal self. This inner sculpting is employed by those committed to succeeding at improving themselves. Our motivation also rises when we blend positive thinking about how we will succeed at change with a recognition of the challenges and setbacks we will face in pursuing change. Your personal change journey will not always be a smooth ride! There will be blind spots, foggy conditions, wrong turns, flat tires...and days when you will simply run out of fuel. But the real "you" that you want to be is too compelling a destination to pass on." (**4**)

The Inside-Out approach to personal leadership development according to Steven R. Covey means, "to start first with self – to start with the most inside part of self – with your paradigms, your character and your motives."

Is it possible that if we go into our inner core and observe life from there, we may become transformed people and therefore, transformational leaders? To create a future, we have to do so by standing in the future. In other words, we look back from the future to the present and do not stand in the present looking towards the future. This can only be accomplished from our inner core. The scriptures inform us that God has "given human beings an awareness of eternity" – Ecclesiastes 3:10 (Jewish Bible).

When we are anchored in our inner core, it expands our inner perception. It brings about powerful change in our lives. As our mind is cleared of the debris of restless thought, it is as though truth and authenticity emerge from hiding and come gradually into sharper focus. We start to see what is central to our existence and what is peripheral. We are not as affected by the changing winds of life. We experience more energy. We pay more attention to others, since we are already at peace with ourselves.

When we live from our inner core, we will develop the foresight that is necessary for leadership. Foresight is a sort of looking out into the realm of possibility that is developed from the inner core. It is critical to effective leadership from the inside-out. On some occasions, it may be thought to defy rational analysis but in fact, many of the features of foresight can propel a leader and those who follow said leader into a prepared future.

Foresight is directly connected to what many believe to be the spiritual or the intuitive. Many prophets and sages are said to be people with foresight. However, we can all operate from that place on some level if we are willing to develop it. Foresight also involves a broader than usual span of awareness, meaning that we become open to perceptions beyond the factual or sensory levels, which is at the level of apprehension or intuition. Foresight releases the ability to integrate or synthesize these diverse inputs and perceptions to come up with an informed response to what the future is revealing to us.

"Foresight along with wisdom requires the harnessing of emotions, thoughts and beliefs so that at critical moments, emotions don't commandeer the more rational parts of our thinking. Foresight is the lead in personal leadership.

Foresight requires the development of a constant and habitual orientation of the mind toward the future. As a leader, the future and what may lie in the future and what you may do in the future, is one of the primary perspectives from which a leader must begin to examine everything that goes on around them." (**5**)

In his book "Understanding Leadership," the author Tom Marshall says that, "foresight also requires certain capacities at the intellectual or rational level, and these need to be consciously applied and developed." He further states that foresight is distinguishable because of the following:

1. It requires developing a constant and habitual orientation of the mind towards the future.

2. It involves acquiring the habit of examining everything and assessing everything in terms of potential and possibilities.

3. It also involves not only the active gathering of information, data, impressions, opinions, insights and hunches but also an instinctive sense for what is relevant and what is not.

4. Associated with this is the capacity for creative thinking – that is, the ability to generate possibilities or ideas that make sense of some or all of the information that has been assembled.

The means by which we can develop this type of foresight is through the identification of our capacities; in other words, what is actually possible to you, for you and through you. Have you been neglecting, misusing or even partially using what you currently have residing in your inner core? How are you endeavoring to increase your capacities in your inner core?

"The key to working from the inside out, the paradigm of primary greatness, is to educate and obey the conscience (or the inner core) – that unique human endowment that senses congruence or disparity with correct principles and lifts us towards them." **(6)**

CHAPTER TWO: REFLECTIONS

Personal Leadership is a state of mind and heart. It asks us to be fully present in our lives, awake to habitual behaviors and willing to look at every situation with fresh eyes.

All real growth and progress is made step-by-step, following a natural sequence of development.

Every human has the instinct and capacity for leadership but most do not have the courage or will to cultivate it.

This process of learning to live from our inner core is a lifelong journey however, we can become better and better at it as we put into practice some basic ideas that can enhance this process.

How do we access our inner core? We access our inner core as our inner core!

To create a future, we have to do so by standing in the future meaning that we look back from the future to the present and not stand in the present looking towards the future.

The Power of Your Purpose

"Where purpose is not known abuse is inevitable."

Dr. Myles Munroe

What would a purpose filled life look like for you? How would you explain it? What would the fulfillment of your purpose look like at the end of this phase of your total existence? The goal of the following exercise is to help you articulate your vision of your purpose filled life (for your remaining years), as seen by you today. You may have given this question a lot of thought, or perhaps only thought of it in narrow career-specific terms. You may also believe that you don't have a firm answer yet to this question and you want to be open to the possibility that your objectives and aspirations may change. The goal of the following exercise is to answer the question in the best and most complete way you can for now, and agree with yourself that you will come back to review and revise this often, as needed. What would the fulfillment of your purpose look like to you? This means that you will have to consider what the future looks like right now. Your future would in this moment become your present. I would like to encourage you to sit down and write out what that might be. Below is a template that you can use.

The year is 20_ _, and on a warm spring evening, you lie down in bed to sleep for one more night of your long and eventful life. You are 120 years old today. You have known over the last few weeks that your remaining days on earth are now a countable few, and on this one evening, your mind drifts into a journey across

the decades of your life...the 2010's, 2020's and beyond...time has flown by faster than you could ever have imagined, but you have reason to be proud and contented with how you lived out each day and each year and each decade, to end up where you are now, in the spring of 20_ _.

There have been challenges and there have been triumphs, but you realize now that the broad course of your life, your strivings and your pursuits, have stayed true to your purpose.

Put yourself in that moment- in the twilight years of your life- and write down what you think would be the kind of life you must have led to allow you to conclude that it was, in fact, a purpose filled life. Try to be as concrete and as specific as you can about the kinds of things that would have needed to happen to make it a purpose filled life for you, as you look back at life on the day you have turned 120.

The purpose of someone is their very reason for existence. According to Dr. Myles Munroe, "true leadership cannot be born or exist without a sense of purpose. Purpose is the discovery of a reason for your existence and is defined as the original intent for the creation of a thing. Every human being was created for a specific purpose, and when that purpose is discovered, then a leader is born." Dr. Munroe further states, "purpose creates a leader because it provides an assignment for life and signals a sense of significance. Your leadership is hidden in your purpose, and your purpose is the key to your passion."

Steven R. Covey was a proponent of the idea of beginning with the end in mind. He would often discuss writing a personal mission statement or a vision statement for our lives. These statements would basically address two things: 1.) What is it your life is about? And 2.) How are you going to go about it? In other words, what is your purpose and what are the principles that you are living by?

Each of us has been given what is necessary for the fulfillment of the purpose for our lives. You may wonder how that can be?

All humans have God-given endowments. We may not all begin with these endowments at the same starting point, but we all have them in one form or another. What we do with them will determine whether or not we will fulfill the purpose for our lives. The first endowment is that we have been "**made in the image of God**" (Genesis 1:26). Being made in the image of God means that you and I have within us everything needed to complete the assignments that we have been given. If we were not equipped with the necessary components to fulfill the purpose given to us, then it would be unjust to expect us to do so. So the presupposition we can begin with is that, since we have been given life, we have a purpose and since we have a purpose, we have what is needed to fulfill that purpose. Each of us must travel the road to self-discovery, and we will find what we need on that road.

The idea of being made in the image of God raises another critical question: what does God look like? Does God look like all of us or do all of us look like God? The reality is that no one besides Jesus Christ has seen God, so none of us knows what God looks like. "No one has ever seen God, but the one and only Son, who is himself God and is in closet relationship with the Father, has made him known" (John 1:18). Therefore, we are not looking for an image of someone we are to tap into the essence of someone that is all encompassing, all surpassing and that completely engulfs our entire existence. Then and only then can we live in a connected way to the purpose that we have been given.

The second endowment is **"life and awareness."** Life is the body of earthly matter being brought into existence from the infinite. It is not just life like we might find in an animal it is cognition and cause. We become the cause of what ultimately effects, us through our thinking, speaking and acting. This is the responsibility that we must all assume to fulfill our purpose. These are gifts from God. Our awareness is really our awakening. It is the awakening to the eternal and the infinite. As we awaken to life we become aware of an unlimited supply from God for the fulfillment of any purpose we have been given. Everything we need to fulfill our purpose is within us and those connected to us for that purpose.

The third great endowment   is **"free will."** Free will in this context simply means that we have the ability and choice to choose to do what we want to do with the intellect, gifts, talents and abilities we have been given. There is an accountability component to these choices, meaning that we must answer for how our intellect, our gifts, talents and abilities are ultimately used. We are also accountable for the development of these gifts, talents and abilities. They have been given to us as our own for the usage of the fulfillment of purpose. Therefore, to the extent that we are committed to the development of these gifts, talents and abilities, we will work towards that end. Free will is actually governed by the laws that govern our purpose. Yes, we can choose things contrary to our purpose in life; however, the consequences of those choices would be most sincerely detrimental. It would take us outside of the scope of our reason for existence. On the other hand, when we use our 'free will' to operate in concert with the Creator's design for our lives we become an unstoppable force of life.

PERSONAL LEADERSHIP LESSON

One of the most frequently asked questions that I have received from people is, "how do I discover the purpose for my life?" You don't have to look any further than within yourself. We are born because of our purpose and therefore, our purpose is always within us. The times that I have operated at less than my best in leadership have been those occasions when I have not exercised the awareness of what my true purpose in that instance was.

There are more than seven billion people residing on planet earth at the time of this writing. I don't think that it would be to, broad of an assumption for me to say that most of us have lost touch with our divine purpose for life or have not even remotely come close to connecting with it. Discovering that purpose within each of us is our spirit's purpose within our purpose. I believe the incarnation of Jesus Christ to be more than just a rescue mission of humanity, even though it was that. I believe that it was also a mission to re-introduce humanity to their true essence and nature. For you and I are indeed a creation of the Creator and when we awaken to the realization that we are children of God we will only desire to fulfill the greatness within each of us.

James Giles in his book, "The Essence of Greatness" lists several key principles of greatness. They are as follows:

1. Know your intrinsic value.

2. Know that you have a purpose for being alive.

3. Discover your purpose.

4. Decide to fulfill your purpose.

5. Decide not to be mediocre.

6. Dream of what you can do.

7. Become a master of what you do.

8. Share what you know!

9. Never stop learning and growing!

10. Think generationally!!

11. Don't practice defiance for its own sake, but when necessary march to the beat of your own drummer.

12. Draw from the power of the Holy Spirit in you.

13. Make wise use of your time.

14. Develop strong listening skills.

15. Read one non-fiction book each month related to your area of interest!!!!!

16. Find mentors.

17. Practice the power of prayer.

18. Visualize your success.

19. Record God's exploits in and through you for posterity; this journal may someday become your memoirs!

20. Work long, hard and smart!

Learning to live from the inside out begins with our core beliefs. At the top of that list   must be the belief that people are born with a purpose. In fact, the moniker for each of our lives must be "I will discover and live my purpose." The essence of the idea is that we are not fully engaged and authentic until we begin to operate from our purpose. We perform better as leaders when we live in harmony with our authentic selves. Aligned with that is our belief in focusing on strengths and managing our weaknesses.

This is accomplished through the development of daily practices. Like a professional athlete, if a leader lacks the discipline of practice, all the talent in the world will not lead to success.

Living from the context of a purpose also entails leaders and emerging leaders learning to live our lives in such a way where our lives are foretelling what is to come. A life that is deeply entrenched in the desire to be what the Creator has designed for us to be will move us beyond a time frame and into a legacy which I believe to be the embodiment of a purpose. Our passion must therefore be to live in such a way that those who follow us are moved to join themselves to our work, in their own unique way.

We are created with a need for purpose and meaning in life. We want to make a contribution to someone or something that is meaningful to us. However, some of the things that we engage in don't provide us with any intrinsic contentment or contribute constructively to the culture. This is because inherent in our purpose is meaning that what we are involved with does matter, the relationships that we have are important and our sense of contribution to something meaningful is satisfying in and of itself.

If you have found it difficult to discover your purpose in life, there are a series of questions that I would like to encourage you to answer that I believe can assist you in beginning that journey. They are:

1. What do you see as your contribution in life?

2. What is the purpose in what you do?

3. Who are the people that have and continue to inspire you?

4. What are the qualities that you look for in a close friend?

5. What are your unique skills and talents?

6. What are the best qualities you express in a personal relationship?

How would you complete this statement…**My mission behind everything that I do is_____?**

One of the primary purposes for leadership is to bring about transformation. It is learning to lead from the internal to the external from being reactive to being proactive. "People with an understanding of their purpose recognize that they don't have a job rather they have an assignment or a divine purpose." (**1**)

CHAPTER THREE: REFLECTIONS

The purpose of someone is their very reason for existence.

"Purpose creates a leader because it provides an assignment for life and signals a sense of significance. Your leadership is hidden in your purpose, and your purpose is the key to your passion."

We are not looking for an image of someone we are to tap into the essence of someone that is all encompassing, all surpassing and that completely engulfs our entire existence.

Living from the context of a purpose also entails leaders and emerging leaders learning to live our lives in such a way where our lives are foretelling what is to come.

Your Guiding Values

**"Your beliefs become your thoughts, Your thoughts become
your words, Your words become your actions,
Your actions become your habits, Your habits become
your values, Your values become
your destiny."**

Mahatma Gandhi

One of the most comprehensive definitions that I have heard of what principles are comes from Steven R. Covey in his book entitled, "Principle-Centered Leadership." He says, "principles are not invented by us or society; they are the laws of the universe that pertain to human relationships and human organizations. They are part of the human condition, consciousness and conscience. To the degree that people recognize and live in harmony with such basic principles as fairness, equity, justice, integrity, honesty, and trust, they move toward either survival and stability on the one hand or disintegration and destruction on the other."

He also states that, "correct principles are like compasses: they are always pointing the way. Principles are self-evident, self-validating natural, *universal,* (italics added) laws. They don't change or shift. Principles apply at all times in all places. Principles, unlike values, are objective and external. Values are subjective and internal. Values are like maps. When people align their personal values with correct principles, they are liberated from old perceptions or paradigms." (**1**)

In the practical sense, principles, which are universal truths that are overarching, have to be contextualized. They are contextualized in and through our personal value systems. Our values are lived out in human spheres like our relationships (i.e. family, social, personal), our parenting, our education, our citizenship, our careers, and our overall well-being amongst other areas.

For leaders and emerging leaders, we are often left with the impression that "remarkable leaders—people with passion, commitment, courage—people who stand for a particular result while it is still a possibility, empower themselves to act, and make their vision real." Somewhere we know that those qualities of leadership are available to us as well, but the way we usually think of leaders builds in a certain distance. We think that certain leaders are somehow different—that they're born with some special gift that sets them apart, that makes them be extraordinary.

To assume that leaders just started out as extraordinary, however, is to overlook what it took along the way to get them to where they are. More importantly, those views about leadership can limit our own access to being effective leaders. When we think of ourselves as being a particular way, with characteristics and traits that are "set" or "fixed," we block that access. If asked, we might explain these fixed notions of ourselves based on whatever opportunities and experiences we did or didn't have, decisions we did or didn't make, the luck of the draw." (2) However, we do have a say about who we are and who we can be. Should we choose to be a leader, to take a stand, to fulfill a vision, we have full access to doing so. There are the principles that pertain to everyone we simply need the mechanism to begin to live out the values that positively impact those we are leading.

Let's begin with the macro components of principles and move to the micro components of principles that are systematically lived out through our values. Everything in the universe is governed by principles. You and I are included in that everything. These principles are in operation in every experience of our lives. It doesn't matter who we are or where we have come from, they are not only relevant to us but they also have mastery over all aspects of our lives. They are unbreakable and unchangeable. They are inevitable. For instance, the law of gravity is at work in and over our lives every moment of every day, whether we acknowledge it or not. Its influence extends beyond the earth to other planets. It is what makes the planets orbit the stars. Yet, if at any moment we choose to not cooperate with that law we will know it immediately. We cannot technically violate a law because it is universally and eternally fixed. We can either cooperate with it or not. This is the expansive influence and the nature of principles or universal laws.

There are principles that govern everything on every level – spiritually, mentally, and physically. God has given us principles or universal laws so that we can manifest our highest potential. They are not intended to work against us rather they are there to enhance us.

How do we begin to integrate an understanding of principles to create a value system that empowers us to be effective leaders? There is an aligning process that we must engage in to see this take place on a practical level. We need to have an understanding of what our primary motivation is at the center of our lives. If we do not have a clear sense of what our foundation is, then it will be a little more difficult to lead out from values that are meaningful for others. Our guiding principles cannot only be goals; they must become our values. Our values need to become a living, breathing reality in our lives.

Our values have to be cultivated because we will frequently be challenged by the power of past habits to live based upon the attainment of previous goals. It is a commitment that we must intentionally make to ourselves.

PERSONAL LEADERSHIP LESSON

In my own life I experienced a challenge in how the power of past habits can adversely affect our leadership. I had experienced a number of years of what many would have considered success in my leadership endeavors. I was a community leader in my city and I had developed a good reputation abroad. However, my own idea of that success led me to make a series of decisions that ultimately were detrimental to my leadership position. In the attempt to maintain certain appearances, I violated the fundamental principles that made up my value system. I began to make decisions out of the context of previous goals that I had attained. The image of success had become more important to me than the actual attainment of success in the fulfillment of my vision. As a result, I had to begin to re-examine why there was a gap of sorts between what I thought that I valued and the way that I was not living out those values. It was a trying time and the understanding of myself that I gained from those experiences I believe is assisting me in being an even more effective leader than previously.

In a written exercise given by Dr. Steve Hayes, we can learn to close the gap between our current lives and the values we are growing in. According to Dr. Hayes, values are not specific goals, but general life directions. As we look at them we can then later translate these values into concrete goals. If you find yourself writing down material things that can be obtained such as an object, stop and rethink what it is you are asking for; that is, directions that can always be pursued and made to manifest, but that can never be fully obtained or finished.

Read through the following list of ten common values given to us by Dr. Hayes and think about your personal values in each of these ten categories. Then, write down your personal values in each domain.

As you work through this exercise, you may discover that certain domains are very important to you and others are not. It's not as though you need to value each of these different areas of life to the same degree. Different people have different values. For the moment, try to find a value that you hold in each domain. If there is any area for which you really can't think of anything, it's okay to skip it.

Be careful that you don't base this exercise on what you think your friends, family, or societal expectations are. Write about what you value. Be honest and open and give yourself the opportunity to fully explore what you value.

1. Marriage/Intimate Relationship

For most people, intimate relationships are very important. This is the relationship you have with your spouse. If you are not in such a relationship right now, you can still answer these questions in terms of what you aspire to find in such a relationship.

What kind of person would you most like to be in the context of an intimate relationship? It might help to think about specific actions you would like to take, and then use those to dig down to the underlying motives for such actions. What are those underlying motives? How do they reflect what you value in your relationships? Do not put down goals (like "getting married"); you can specify your associated goals later.

2. Parenting

Think about what it means to you to be a mother or a father. What would you like to be about in this role? If you don't have children, you can still answer this question. What do you want to be about in supporting this role in others?

3. Family Relations (Other Than Intimate Relations and Parenting)

This domain is about family, not about your husband or wife or children, but about other areas of family life. Think about what it means to be a son, daughter, brother, sister, aunt, uncle, cousin, grand-parent, or in-law. What would you like to be about in your family relationships? You may think about this broadly or only in terms of your nuclear family. What values would you like to see manifest in your life in this area?

4. Friendship/Social Relations

Friendships are another area of personal relations that most people value. What kind of friend would you like to be? Think about your closest friends and see if you can connect with what you would like to have manifest in your life regarding your friends.

5. Career/Employment

Work and careers are important for most people because that area is where a great deal of your life is spent. Whether your work is humble or grand, the question of values in work is important. What kind of an employee do you most want to be? What do you want to stand for in your work? What kind of a difference do you want to make through your job or your business?

6. Education/Training/Personal Growth and Development

This area can cover all kinds of learning and personal develop-ment. School-based education is one. But this area includes all the things you do to learn, as well. What type of learner do you want to be? What aspects of personal growth are important for you to pursue; what would you like to have manifest in your life?

7. Recreation/Leisure

Recreation, leisure, and relaxation are important to most of us. It is in those areas that we recharge our batteries; these activities are often where we connect with family and friends. Think about what is meaningful to you about your hobbies, sports, avocations, vacations, and other forms of recreation. In these areas, what would you like to have manifest in your life?

8. Spirituality

By spirituality, we don't necessarily mean organized religion, although that could certainly be included . Spirituality includes everything that helps you feel connected to something larger than yourself, to a sense of wonder and transcendence in life. It includes your faith, spiritual and religious practices, and your connection with others in this domain. What do you most want to be about in this area of your life?

9. Citizenship

How would you like to contribute to society and be a member of the community? What do you really want to be about in social/ political/charitable and community service areas?

10. Health/Physical Well-Being

We are spiritual and physical beings, and taking care of our bodies and our health through diet, exercise, and sound health practices is another important domain. What do you want to have manifest in your life in these areas?

To test your values, look over what you have written and ask yourself the following question in regard to each of the values you wrote down: "If no one knew that I was working on this, would I still do it?" For instance, if you desire a certain type of personal achievement, ask yourself, "Let me imagine that I had the opportunity to pursue this achievement, but I could not tell anyone about what I achieve. Would I still devote myself to achieving it?" or "What if my family would never know I achieved this. Would I still value it?" If you find that you have written down statements that don't ring true, or are more a matter of attempting to live up to someone else's external standards, than stating what is truly in your heart, go back and edit what you wrote. This list is not for anyone else. It is for you.

If you ever find yourself getting off of track in the integration of your values in your daily life, it is important to take concrete steps to close the gap. We can train our minds to be focused when we are pursuing our values and we can push ourselves to do so when we are not. As time goes on, our character will be remolded into the type of person that we know that we can and want to be. This can be called a re-sculpting process.

Today, I am an example of this re-sculpting process. I have been in a position where I lost everything as a leader and sunk to the lowest levels of life. I discuss this further in my book, "I Found." At the same time, I am an example that sometimes the way that your highest values are attained are learned both from what not to do as well as how to do things in the proper manner.

CHAPTER FOUR: REFLECTIONS

Principles are not invented by us or society; they are the laws of the universe that pertain to human relationships and human organizations.

Principles are like compasses: they are always pointing the way.

Principles are self-evident, self-validating natural, *universal,* (italics added) laws. They don't change or shift.

Principles apply at all times in all places.

God has given us principles or universal laws so that we can manifest our highest potential. They are not intended to work against us; rather they are there to enhance us.

Our guiding principles cannot only be goals they must become our values. Our values need to become a living, breathing reality in our lives.

Self-Management Is A Principle

"If you cannot manage yourself, you have no business managing others."

Gerald Weinberg

C an you remember a time or times in your life when you have been the happiest, most productive, and most successful? Now think about how you would be if you performed from that disposition consistently! This is not impossible. Consistently functioning at your optimum in a given situation is almost always related to strong self-management, and when you recognize the self-managing strategies behind your best achievements, you can begin to use them more often. Everyone is a self-manager, at least some of the time. But few people are self-managers fully, consistently, or systematically.

As a self-manager, you will at some point need to address every aspect of your life, developing and committing to practical strategies for growth and improvement. Do you really believe that you can attain greater personal and professional fulfillment? It is not a matter of comparing yourself against anyone or anything else. It is actually learning to surrender to the best aspects of yourself and learning to implement those aspects consistently into your life. It is an adjustment in thinking before it becomes an adjustment in behavior. Self-management skills will make you more organized, more productive, more satisfied, and more personally fulfilled.

Maturation in the area of self-management begins to take place with the realization that "No one is coming to the rescue." Everything you are or ever will be is entirely up to you. This life is not a dress rehearsal for anything else. This is the real thing. All of our decisions and indecisions, our actions and inactions, have added up to create the life we are living at this very minute. If we want things to be different in the future, we will have to make things different in the present. We will have to take complete charge of ourselves and our lives and make things change, because they won't change by themselves.

In relationship to leadership, self-management is not something that is developed because someone is a leader. It is about being intentional about creating a future that we are out to create not based on any actuality, but based on the stand we take for having that future happen. It is something each of us can bring to that with which we are involved—our day-to-day lives, our families, our communities, our nations. Leaders are ordinary women and men who dare to be related to possibilities bigger than themselves, attracted by the world that's opened up by their vision and their commitment.

Self-management is really personal management, time management, life management. When we recognize that we are a treasure of resources wrapped in a person, we will also better understand that all that we need to fulfill our assignment is already inside of us. This treasure must first be discovered. It is made up of our experiences, and our relationships. You can benefit from this idea by standing back and looking at yourself in terms of who you are, instead of what you do. We tend to define ourselves in terms of our work, in terms of what we are spending most of our time doing at the present moment. The fact is that you are not just what you do. You are much more than this.

Each of us has the combination of ingredients that makes us a unique and remarkable human being, different from anyone else who ever has lived or whoever will live. We all have undergone a wide variety of experiences, both positive and negative. We each have a unique intelligence, much of which is not yet developed to the fullest. We also have skills that we have acquired through hard work, education both formal and informal, discipline and practice.

You have abilities that you were born with, which makes it easy for you to do certain jobs and to accomplish certain tasks. You have energy and ambition and goals and opportunities. You have a philosophy of life, however developed it is, and you have attitudes and perspectives that make you extraordinary.

As the psychologist Abraham Maslow once wrote, "The story of the human race is the story of men and women selling themselves short." The average person tends to settle for far less than they are capable of and then wonders why they are so dissatisfied and frustrated with their lives.

PERSONAL LEADERSHIP LESSON

I know this feeling well. At a certain point in my life, I became a person who settled for less than my best. Someone once said, "none of us has the right to do less than our best." However, when I began to feel like I was settling for much less than the God-given potential that I had, I found myself not managing my life in ways that I had previously. For twenty plus years I had lived a disciplined life in the areas of personal and corporate accountability. Then after those twenty years, I became short-sighted and made decisions without the level of accountability that I needed to continue to grow in the area of self-management. Self-management is not something that can be theorized. It is not a stagnant process, but it is dynamic and engaging. It is something that we must make a consistent commitment to growing in. This does require being accountable to others in this process. In that instance, I realized that I was not being accountable for my self-management development. As a result, instead of recognizing this I chose rather to continue to attempt to fix things that I had damaged without the assistance of others. That didn't work and it caused further challenges in my life which

ultimately led to me having to step away from my leadership position for a number of years. This was a result of the lack of self-management.

The premise behind self-management is that we are engaging in taking an active and conscious role in examining whether or not our lives are moving towards the fulfillment of something larger than ourselves. Leaders are ordinary men and women who dare to be related to possibilities bigger than themselves, attracted by the world that is opened up by their vision and their commitment. When we create a future through a vision and invest ourselves in it, that future starts to open up new territory. It gives birth to, what it attracts.

More than thirty years ago, management scholars Fred Luthans and Tim Davis suggested: "research and writing in the management field have given a great deal of attention to managing societies, organizations, groups, and individuals. Strangely, almost no one has paid any attention to managing oneself more effectively.... Self-management seems to be a basic prerequisite for effective management of other people, groups, organizations and societies."

Self-management represents an individual exerting control over some aspect of his or her decision-making and selected behaviors. To do this, the person must define specific behaviors related to identified goals and take appropriate action. Self-regulation has been evaluated in laboratory and clinical settings. Positive results have been found with many behaviors.

Training in self-management teaches people to assess their present location in life, to set specific goals in response to where they are in life, to monitor ways in which the environments they are consistently in facilitates or hinders goal attainment, and to identify or administer reinforcements for working towards, the attainment of those goals. In essence, being trained in self-management teaches people skills in self-observation, to compare their current behaviors with goals that they set, and to administer the changes needed to bring about and sustain goal commitment.

There are four specific elements that can assist us in managing ourselves. These elements are drawn from a study on "Effective Self-Management Techniques," studied by C.W. Von Bergen, Barlow Soper and Buddy Gaster." (**1**)

Element 1 — Self-Assessment and Reality Check

Self-assessment, requires individuals to carefully analyze what they perceive to be their own abilities, competencies, weaknesses, skills, interests, values, and goals. After such an evaluation, an individual should identify what needs are realistic. This may be accomplished through a personality assessment process or talking with friends, colleagues, or relatives who have a reputation for providing honest, candid feedback. It is interesting that the management guru Peter Drucker suggested working on one's strengths: "one should waste as little effort as possible on improving areas of low competence. It takes far more energy and work to improve from incompetence to mediocrity than it takes to improve from first-rate performance to excellence. And yet most people—especially most teachers and organizations—concentrate on making incompetent performers into mediocre ones. Energy, resources, and time should go instead to making a competent person into a star performer."

Element 2 — Goal Setting and Action Planning

To address this step, we have to first establish a measurable goal. It needs to be specific, but challenging. This goal is typically called a distant goal in that it is relatively far off from the desired behavior. When we have a goal that is not very far away it is called a proximal goal. It must be noted that the proximal goal is very specific and does not necessarily include research, or discussions with colleagues.

Once measurable goals have been set, the need to develop an action plan to achieve this outcome is important. In effect, the goal setting process must incorporate an action taking component, energized with the intention to reduce the gap between the initial situation and targeted outcomes.

Element 3 — Constructive Thought Patterns

The next step in the self-management process is adapted from the sports psychology literature and suggests that before beginning a task and while performing it, individuals should engage in positive (constructive) thoughts about that activity and its accomplishment. In particular, individuals are more motivated and better prepared to accomplish a task after they have engaged in self-talk and positive mental imagery. Self-talk refers to any situation in which we talk to ourselves about our own thoughts or actions. It can create positive expectations and thereby raises motivation and subsequent performance. For example, research found that young skaters who received self-talk training improved their performance one year later. Mental imagery refers to mentally picturing a task and imagining successfully performing it beforehand. While an aspect of mental imagery is that it may help us anticipate possible errors, it also involves visualizing successful completion of the task. Research has shown that visualization can enhance actual sports performance, and encouraging this strategy has now become a widespread coaching technique. Visualization can be applied to business or even work situations to enhance one's own achievements in business or work. For example, visualization may be particularly helpful for those individuals giving a speech or having a conversation. Here individuals are encouraged to engage in mental rehearsal by visualizing themselves delivering the speech in a very effective manner. Peak performers are visualizers.

Both self-talk and mental imagery can be said to lead to hope. "Having hope means believing you have both the will and the way to accomplish your goals, whatever they may be. Hope has proven a powerful predictor of outcome in many studies that have been done. In a study of 3,920 students at the University of Kansas at the turn of the century it was found that the amount of hope among entering freshmen was more predictive of academic success than either high school grades or SAT scores, the two conventional predictors. Data suggests people with high hopes tend to be reality centered, set higher goals for themselves, and actively work to attain their expectations. In short, they were highly motivated.

Element 4 — Self-Monitoring

Self-monitoring is the process of keeping track of one's progress toward a goal and is a key component of the self-management process. One of the keys is to make the monitoring process as effortless as possible, and to monitor and record performance in some manner. Another key component in self-monitoring is that we have to establish a process that is natural and easy to do. "Many studies show that if you get someone to be more aware of what they are doing, they'll be better at it, virtually without exception."

All leaders have a basic philosophy that they are operating from. This philosophy flows out of their shared experiences in life. As J. Robert Clinton states, "we all have processing items in our lives, whether in terms of spiritual formation (character building)," or functional formation (skills that we have developed to lead). "These lessons form a growing reservoir of wisdom that leaders use in the future. Some lessons are more explicit; others are implicit."

When it comes to self-management, we must remember that taking personal responsibility for our lives is of the utmost importance. Responsibility is our ability to make the types of decisions we need to make as our response to a particular circumstance. This creates a sense of self-mastery. To practice self-mastery there are several key areas that we must look at.

The first area is self-discipline. Dr. Myles Munroe in his book entitled, "The Spirit of Leadership," informs us that "discipline may be defined as self-imposed standards and restrictions motivated by a desire that is greater than the alternatives. It is self-policing." The practice of self-discipline must become just that, a practice. Someone once said, that "practice doesn't make perfect, practice makes permanent." Whatever we commit ourselves to do repeatedly and aggressively becomes habit in our lives. Self-discipline begins when we are "regulated by a code of conduct in keeping with a set of goals and commitments dictated by an intended result." (Munroe – 2) The ongoing result of self-discipline is self-transformation. When we exercise the kind of control over our appetites and emotions the results that we will reap will be transformative. Another way that Dr. Munroe discusses this idea of transformation is when he states, "he/she who cannot control his/her thoughts will never control themselves; he/she who cannot rule themselves will never control life; he/she who cannot control himself/herself will be controlled by others." Self-discipline is foundational to a leaders' entire life.

The second area is time management. I often tell people that time is one of my best friends. Why, you may ask? It is because time waits for no one and time reveals all. We cannot get around time, yet we can live our lives in such a way where we are functioning beyond time. Time management is really self-management. Each of us have been given the same amount of time each day, each week and each month. Therefore, time management is learning to master the time apportioned to each of us.

"The essence of time management is to set priorities and then to organize and execute around them. Setting priorities requires us to think carefully and clearly about values, about ultimate concerns. These then have to be translated into long – and short-term goals and plans and translated once more into schedules or time slots. Then, unless something more important – not something more urgent – comes along, we must discipline ourselves to do as we planned." (3) Everyone, of us has to learn to budget our time. There are some essential activities that would benefit us as we learn to utilize our time properly. Those activities include, "work and associated aspects; rest, relaxation, and sleep; recreation – mental and physical; development of mental and physical abilities; eating; social activities; and spiritual activities, study and time for self." (**4**)

The third area   is   simplicity. We are living in an era where we have many opportunities to simplify our lives. Yet it seems that the lives of people are becoming more and more complex even with the advancement of technology. Simplicity is the state, quality, or an instance of being simple. It is freedom from complexity…absence of pretentiousness, ornament; plainness; absence of complication. In another instance complexity means to be convoluted, confusing, entangled, compounded, elaborate, tangled, tortuous, mixed-up…etc.

There are key drivers of complexity in this digital world. We have social media, mobile applications which have resulted in an explosion of choices in terms of products and services. These drivers are generally influenced by cultural expectations through its measurements of success and the external pressures to maintain the status quo. Complexity is growing and many don't have the ability to maintain the pace. The way to deal with complexity is to focus on the inward journey.

Professor Hitendra Wadhwa, gives us some important principles in moving our lives towards simplicity. He states that,

1. Simplicity ultimately drives success in life.

2. We must condense things down to their essence.

3. Simplicity is the opposite of being simple-minded.

4. Simplicity must be embraced as a core principle in life to live successfully.

5. We must infuse simplicity into our actions, words, thoughts, feelings and identity.

6. The Principle of Simplicity:

    a. If Simplicity is about doing and thinking in the simplest of terms…what's the simplest you can ever be?

b. The more we understand and master these principles, the more effective we can be in achieving our goals.

c. There is value in learning to master one thing and delivering that to others.

d. The Principles of Inner Mastery –

　　i. Divide things to the lowest/smallest common denominator.

　　ii. Take small steps every day to grow in simplicity.

　　iii. Do high-frequency practice – Practice makes permanent.

　　iv. Get constructive feedback.

　　v. Learn from top performers.

The fourth area is intentional change. Can you identify one thing that you would really like to change about yourself? What would you identify as the main barrier(s) you face making this change? Why do people not change? Why do we often fail at our efforts to change? Someone once said, "Men (people) often become what they believe themselves to be. If I believe I cannot do something, it makes me incapable of doing it. But when I believe I can, then I acquire the ability to do it even if I did not have the ability in the beginning."

How much can you or I change? The real question is what aspect(s) of ourselves are we actually open to change? Which aspect(s) of ourselves are we not open to change? The new science indicates that

epigenetics which is the ability to supersede any genetic malfunction allows us to go beyond our own strengths and weaknesses. In addition, the new science of neuroplasticity indicates that the brain is regenerating and can constantly expand its capacity through learning new ideas.

The new science informs us that we can acquire entirely different skill sets in areas that we did not previously have them when we apply ourselves to consistent learning and discovery.

According to Dr. Myles Munroe, "there is nothing more secure than the familiar. There is nothing as constant as change. Change is inevitable. Change is the essence of life. The essence of change is growth, because growth is change. As long as something is living it is growing. As long as something is growing, it is changing. The only alternative is death." He goes on further to say that change always has a price tag. All you can really do with change is manage it. God's will is not that you are changed by change, rather that you dream, plan and execute change. Crisis management is a term for those who don't manage change. You must change intentionally.

You can only change the changeable. You must adapt to the unchangeable. Change is the motivator of progress.

1. There are three types of change:

   • Those that happen around you – fashions; society.

   • Those that happen to you – natural aging.

   • Those that you make happen.

2. There are three types of people when it comes to change:

   • Those who watch what happens.

   • Those who ask what happened?

   • Those who make things happen.

It is not what happens to you that ultimately matters, it is what you do about what happens to you that ultimately matters."

CHAPTER FIVE: REFLECTIONS

Consistently functioning at your optimum in a given situation is almost always related to strong self-management — and when you recognize the self-managing strategies behind your best achievements, you can begin to use them more often.

Maturation in the area of self-management begins to take place with the realization that "No one is coming to the rescue."

All of our decisions and indecisions, our actions and inactions, have added up to create the life we are living at this very minute.

Self-management is really personal management, time management, life management.

The premise behind self-management is that we are engaging in taking an active and conscious role in examining whether or not our lives are moving towards the fulfillment of something larger than ourselves.

Men (people) often become what they believe themselves to be. If I believe I cannot do something, it makes me incapable of doing it. But when I believe I can, then I acquire the ability to do it even if I did not have the ability in the beginning.

CHAPTER SIX

The Power of Paradox

"How wonderful that we have met with a paradox. Now we have some hope of making progress."

Niels Bohr

As human beings, we are naturally designed to solve problems by implementing the right solutions. However, paradoxes are a little more difficult to explain and still remain solution oriented. This is particularly the case when it comes to leaders and leadership. Paradoxes consist of seemingly opposites that do not appear to be able to coexist, however, they do. One of the greatest challenges that a leader will face is the juxtaposition of a set of seemingly contradictory concepts that reveal a hidden and/or unexplained truth. The paradox may be difficult to believe, yet usually the apparent contradiction can be reconciled to a deeper truth in the life of a leader. There are many different paradox definitions depending on the field of endeavor in which it is used.

There are also many famous quotes that also contain paradoxes for instance:

1. "Whatever you do will be insignificant, but it is very important that you do it." – Mahatma Gandhi

2. "Life is a preparation for the future; and the best preparation for the future is to live as if there were none." – Albert Einstein

3. "I know one thing: that I know nothing." – Socrates (via Plato)

4. "Whoever wants to be great among you must be your servant." – Jesus Christ

A number of people are uncomfortable with paradox, including leaders. We tend to want "either/ors" in life instead of "both/ands." We generally want one process or one key that solves all problems and we generally struggle with the contrasts we see around us that we think are irreconcilable. We must understand that God works by attacking the problem or challenges we face in life from both sides at the same time. Our responsibility becomes to continue to move in the direction that we need to be going in while facing a paradox. It is also our responsibility to seek for the greater truth beneath the surface of the paradox.

As a leader or emerging leader, we must learn from the contrasts that we experience in life. We have many natural examples of contrasting ideas or concepts, from light and darkness to male and female coexisting. Paradoxes exist to give us the opportunity to expand our thinking in certain areas beyond the limitations of what we currently understand. They are also able to assist us in exploring certain situational complications and the extent of human judgment. Paradoxes are sometimes situations in which someone thinks that they are in need of something that can only be had by not being in need of it. This has been called a Catch-22, a phrase coined by author Joseph Heller.

The term paradox is from the Greek word "paradoxon" which means, contrary to expectations, existing belief or perceived opinion. It is a statement that appears to be self-contradictory or even absurd to some but it may include a latent truth for us to discover. It is also used to illustrate an opinion or a statement contrary to accepted traditional ideas. I believe the goal of a paradox is to cause us to begin to think through an idea or ideology in an innovative way.

Why is a paradox used when a message or an experience can be conveyed in a straightforward and simple manner? Jesus Christ said that the reason He used parables (which were often paradoxical) was because the truth of the parable is seeking for those who were seeking it. In contrast, it is avoiding those who are not interested in seeking it. When he was asked directly why He used parables, He replied, 'You've been given insight into God's kingdom. You know how it works. Not everybody has this gift, this insight; it hasn't been given to them. Whenever someone has a ready heart for this, the insights and understandings flow freely. But if there is no readiness, any trace of receptivity soon disappears. That's why I tell stories: to create readiness, to nudge people toward receptive insight. In their present state they can stare till doomsday and not see it, listen till they're blue in the face and not get it'" (Matthew 13:11-13 Message Bible). I believe that these statements reveal the basic nature of what a paradox is and why they exist in our lives.

When it comes to leadership, paradoxes help to reveal that a leader is a person, and that leadership is an incredibly important function that flows out from the leader. It also reveals that leadership is not a function to be performed in isolation from people. Leadership is not about charisma or personality, but it is a process that can be learned. When people learn the science of leadership, the art of being a leader will naturally flow from them. This is a paradox because many of the prevailing and acceptable ideas about what a leader is and what a leader does don't fit into that paradigm.

It is quite possible that the greatest paradox that a leader will ever face is this, 'within a leader's greatest strength, you can also identify their greatest weakness.' For instance, if your strength is organizational development, you may in turn struggle with being flexible to different ways that could possibly enhance what you already know. If your strength is drive and determination, your weakness could possibly be that you don't listen to others very well and you may not be the best teammate. What if your strength is loyalty? You may be loyal to a fault and unwilling to change or move forward when it may be time to look at an adjustment. What if your strength is your kindness and care for others? Your weakness may be the inability to accept constructive criticism and deal with conflict.

PERSONAL LEADERSHIP LESSON

I experienced a paradoxical encounter when I was faced with a dilemma of challenging myself because my actions were not in alignment with my words. It was the greatest time of growth in my life, even though it was the most uncomfortable. Paradoxes are not intended to be comfortable; they are meant to provide the greatest lessons of our lives.

As the 14th Dalai Lama stated, "we have bigger houses but smaller families; more conveniences, but less time. We have more degrees but less sense; more knowledge but less judgment; more experts, but more problems; more medicines but less healthiness. We've been all the way to the moon and back, but have trouble in crossing the street to meet our new neighbor. We built more computers to hold more copies than ever, but have less real communication; We have become long on quantity, but short on quality. These are times of fast food but slow digestion; Tall men but short characters; Steep profits but shallow relationships. It's a time when there is much in the window, but nothing in the room."

He is simply informing us that we have exercised insufficient means to address the complexities and nuances presented by paradoxical situations. The reality is that the concept of a paradox has moved from the domain of the philosopher to our personal domains.

A paradox is not necessarily a problem, nor is a problem necessarily a paradox. Problems come into our lives to be solved and paradoxes enter our lives to bring clarity and balance. When we don't recognize the difference between the two, we can find ourselves in a difficult place because a paradox is not to be solved whereas, a problem needs to be solved. A problem will come and go; however, a paradox never ceases to exist.

A paradox often centers around a critical issue in life that confronts our underlying assumption that there is only one right way to do something or one right answer to a question. The tension we feel when we do this comes from treating the issue as a problem that can be solved. In reality if the issue is a complex issue whether in our personal lives, our families, our organizations or society in general there are probably no simple resolutions. They cannot be adequately addressed as problems. Problems have solutions that, when implemented, seem to resolve the issues before us. However, a paradox is often a contrary circumstance that needs to be managed over the long term. It will never go away.

We must develop our capacity to address a number of critical paradoxes   if we are going to demonstrate a leadership style that empowers people rather than subjects them to being less than they are capable of being.

Addressing life's challenging paradoxes requires great courage. As a leader, when your existing values collide with functional realities, I encourage you to answer these questions:

1. What is really going on here?

2. Do others have different perspectives on the issues?

3. Can I discuss this matter with someone in confidence?

   • Who will be honest and objective with me?

   • Who will have a perspective different from my own?

   • Who can help me work through my concerns?

4. What am I doing now that is a barrier to success?

5. Is there a difference between the core values of those that I am working with and my core values?

6. Is this difference, if any, the source of the challenges I face?

7. Can I use this challenge as an opportunity to grow?

8. Can I identify an opportunity to make a difference here?

9. What have I learned about myself in this experience? **(1)**

According to Ralph Jacobson, "instead of seeing the unfolding of an issue as a problem to be solved, perhaps the lens of paradox opens a more productive dialogue and results in greater possibilities for success. What if a disagreement is not someone's fault or what if it isn't a flaw in someone? What if this is a situation in which there are multiple perspectives that are both right and wrong at the same time? What if it wasn't a personal deficiency at all? What if in fact the parties are supposed to have differences? That each from their own perspective is doing what they should." He goes on to say that "the reality is that to be human requires us to deal with paradoxes every day, in most of our human encounters. Leaders spend an inordinate amount of time addressing paradoxical issues." **(2)**

Are there simplified ways of addressing common paradoxes between us and others? There certainly are. One may be to find a trusted and neutral person who can embrace both polarities of the paradox and lead a discussion about them. Secondly, bring together a microcosm of people who represent the various perspectives of the paradox and lead a discussion.

On the wall of Shishu Bhavan, the children's home in Kolkata (formerly known as Calcutta), India that

Mother Teresa founded in 1955, there is a copy of what is called the ten Paradoxical Commandments. They are an adaptation from the original written by Kent Keith. It says,

ANYWAY

People are unreasonable, illogical, and self-centered,

LOVE THEM ANYWAY

If you do good, people will accuse you of selfish, ulterior motives,

DO GOOD ANYWAY

If you are successful, you win false friends and true enemies,

SUCCEED ANYWAY

The good you do will be forgotten tomorrow,

DO GOOD ANYWAY

Honesty, and frankness make you vulnerable,

BE HONEST AND FRANK ANYWAY

What you spent years building may be destroyed overnight,

BUILD ANYWAY

People really need help

but may attack you if you help them,

HELP THEM ANYWAY

Give the world the best you have

And you'll get kicked in the teeth,

GIVE THE WORLD THE BEST YOU'VE GOT ANYWAY

The essential paradox in the life of a leader is the issue of how that person as an individual becomes a multiplicity in others. How do you pour what you have been given into others? I believe this is done by serving them and empowering them in their purposes for life, even through the paradoxes.

CHAPTER SIX: REFLECTIONS

As human beings we are naturally designed to solve problems by implementing the right solutions.

One of the greatest challenges that a leader will face is the juxtaposition of a set of seemingly contradictory concepts that reveal a hidden and/or unexplained truth.

We must understand that God works by attacking the problem or challenges we face in life from both sides at the same time.

As a leader or emerging leader we must learn from the contrasts that we experience in life.

When it comes to leadership, paradoxes help to reveal that a leader is a person and that leadership is an incredibly important function that flows out from the leader.

It is quite possible that the greatest paradox that a leader will ever face is the paradox that, 'within a leader's greatest strength you can also identify their greatest weakness.'

CHAPTER SEVEN

Your Leadership Psyche

**"All learning is remembering. All teaching is reminding.
All lessons are memories, recaptured."**

Neal Donald Walsch

T he word psyche is the Greek term for the soul of a person. It is in reference to the deepest and innermost part of the human being. We call it the heart of the person. It also refers to the essence of the person and the "vital force that animates the body. It is the seat of the feelings, desires, affections, and aversions. It is our very breath." (1)

When a person discovers their leadership calling, it can become the very breath of that person. It can become what they live, eat, sleep and breath all at the same time. It is much the same with many musicians, athletes, scientists, entertainers, and community activists. Something inside of them only finds satisfaction in the thing for which they were born and that which they would freely give of their time and energies.

Can our psyche be enhanced or developed so that we can have optimal function in the area of leadership? Yes, it can! We can learn to develop our emotions and our thoughts when we learn to mobilize our total spiritual, mental and physical resources for any endeavor that we believe in. When we learn to do this, it will not just be a possibility but it will become an inevitable reality demanding constant readiness from us. If we are to be the most effective in our leadership, we must develop a winner's mindset which can surmount great obstacles and which we can learn to re-create the same state of mind at will. We often see professional athletes or musicians do this successfully each time they are required to perform. They train themselves to do this consistently. "For, to become the best person we can each be, we must learn to view ourselves as a composite being with different facets, each of which deserves to achieve its own 'personal best.'" (2)

"He who cannot change the very fabric of his thought will never be able to change reality ..." Anwar Sadat

It must not be beyond the leader or emerging leader to study the basic components of their minds and behaviors and how these work in concert with each other. The theory of multiple intelligences was developed in 1983 by Dr. Howard Gardner, professor of education at Harvard University. It suggests that the traditional notion of intelligence, based on I.Q. testing, is far too limited. Instead, Dr. Gardner proposes eight different intelligences to account for a broader range of human potential in children and adults. These intelligences are:

- **Linguistic intelligence** ("word smart")

- **Logical-mathematical intelligence** ("number/reasoning smart")

- **Spatial intelligence** ("picture smart")

- **Bodily-Kinesthetic intelligence** ("body smart")

- **Musical intelligence** ("music smart")

- **Interpersonal intelligence** ("people smart")

- **Intrapersonal intelligence** ("self-smart")

- **Naturalist intelligence** ("nature smart")

Dr. Gardner says that our schools and culture focus most of their attention on linguistic and logical-mathematical intelligence. We esteem the highly articulate or logical people of our culture. However, Dr. Gardner suggests that we should also place equal attention on individuals who show gifts in the other intelligences: the artists, architects, musicians, naturalists, designers, dancers, therapists, entrepreneurs, and others who enrich the world in which we live. The leadership paradigm will be expanded and more inclusive when we begin to think in these terms. Unfortunately, a number of people who as children had these gifts they didn't receive much reinforcement for them at home or in school. Many of these kids, in fact, end up being labeled "learning disabled," "ADD (attention deficit disorder," or simply underachievers, when their unique ways of thinking and learning aren't addressed by a heavily linguistic or logical-mathematical classroom. The theory of multiple intelligences proposes a major transformation in the way we can be trained as leaders and train other leaders. These lessons can be taught in a wide variety of ways using music, cooperative learning, art, role play, multimedia, travel, inner reflection, and much more. This would certainly expand the opportunity for the leadership potential that I believe is resident in each of us to come out because it would not be limited to only traditional models of leadership development. One of the most remarkable features of the theory of multiple intelligences is how it provides eight different potential pathways to learning.

The theory of multiple intelligences also has strong implications for adult learning and development. Many adults find themselves in jobs or careers that do not make optimal use of their most highly developed intelligences (for example, the highly bodily-kinesthetic individual who is stuck in a linguistic or logical desk-job when he or she would be much happier in a job where they could move around, such as a recreational leader, a forest ranger, or physical therapist). The theory of multiple intelligences gives adults a whole new way to look at their lives, examining potential that they left behind in their childhood (such as a love for art or drama) but now have the opportunity to develop through courses, hobbies, or other programs of self-development.

A further expansion of the multiple intelligence conversation is the more recent study released by Daniel Goleman in his book entitled, "Emotional Intelligence." After years of research about emotional intelligence, brain research and leadership styles scientific evidence showed that a leader's emotional competencies have an enormous impact on the effectiveness of his/her leadership and on the organizations that they lead. Goleman initially detailed 27 competencies which were later refined down to 18 competencies within four emotional intelligence domains. The four dimensions are self-awareness, self-management, social awareness and relationship management. These four competencies were divided further into personal and social competence. The following descriptions of the competencies assist leaders in assessing where they are in the development of their leadership psyche. Not all leaders have all of the competencies; in fact the best leaders may have only strong tendencies in four to six competencies. The areas as summarized by M. Kern concerning the book Emotional Intelligence are below:

Self-Awareness

- Emotional self-awareness: Leaders high in emotional self-awareness are attuned to their inner signals, recognizing how their feelings affect them and their performance.

- Accurate self-assessment: Leaders who know their strengths and limitations can exhibit a sense of humor about themselves.

- Self-confidence: Knowing their strengths allows leaders to play to their strengths.

Self-Management

- Self-control: Leaders with emotional self-control find ways to manage their disturbing emotions and impulses, and channel them in useful ways.

- Transparency: Leaders who are transparent live their values.

- Adaptability: Leaders who are adaptable can juggle multiple demands without losing their focus or energy, and are comfortable with the ambiguities of organizational life.

- Achievement: Leaders with strength in achievement have high personal standards that drive them to seek performance improvements both for themselves and those they lead.

- Initiative: These are leaders who have a sense of efficacy that they have what it takes to control their own destiny.

- Optimism: A leader who is optimistic can roll with the punches seeing an opportunity rather than a threat in a setback.

Social Awareness

- Empathy: Leaders with empathy are able to attune to a wide range of emotional signals, letting them sense the felt, but unspoken, emotions in a person or a group.

- Organizational awareness: A leader with social awareness can be politically astute, able to detect crucial social networks and read key power relationships.

- Service: Leaders high in service competence foster an emotional climate so that people in direct touch with others will keep the relationship on the right track.

Relationship Management

- Inspiration: Leaders who inspire both create resonance and move people with a compelling vision or shared mission.

- Influence: Indicators of a leader's powers of influence range from finding just the right appeal for a given listener to knowing how to build buy-in from key people and a network of support for an initiative.

- Developing others: Leaders who are adept at cultivating people's abilities show a genuine interest in those they are helping along, understanding their goals, strengths, and weaknesses.

- Change catalyst: Leaders who can catalyze change are able to recognize the need for change, challenge the status quo, and champion the new order.

- Conflict management: Leaders who manage conflicts best are able to draw out all parties, understanding the differing perspectives and find a common ideal that everyone can endorse.

- Teamwork and collaboration: Leaders who are able team players generate an atmosphere of friendly collegiality and are themselves models of respect, helpfulness and cooperation.

PERSONAL LEADERSHIP LESSSON

I am not sure enough time is spent on the development of a leader's mental well-being. Leaders are people who often face a tremendous amount of pressure. It is important to me that leaders not only work on their leadership capacities and their physical attributes, but also their mental wellness.

In order to change our perceptions and operate effectively in these various competencies, it is important and necessary to learn how to control and divert our attention. What we give our attention to is the major form in which our consciousness exists. It has been said, "attention is directed consciousness." (**3**) Some are using the word energy for attention today. This is because it has been scientifically proven that energy exists in all aspects of our existence. By directing our energy, we are thereby directing our consciousness towards what we are giving our attention to. It is important to recognize that the maturity of our psyche is directly measured by the degree to which we can direct our own energy. In measurable terms it has been scientifically proven that "all winners have at least one thing in common: an ability to concentrate their attention on a single focus for a long time." (**4**) As we grow in this discipline we can learn more and more how to submit our attention to our will. "Concentration is all-important to achievement because it adds power to any effort, mental or physical. Many successful leaders are notorious for their ability to envelop themselves within a cocoon of concentration. They have an increased awareness of the object of their concentration, along with a decreased awareness of everything else." (**5**)

In his seminal work, "Red Gold," author Grigori Raiport shows us how to modify our psyche at the personality level. First he says that we must detect and minimize our negative identifications. In other words, he encourages us to identify where we have allowed dominant negative aspects of our lives to define who we are. Whether you have ever identified yourself as an angry person, a pessimist, a stressed out person, or a person filled with anxiety, you must detach your personality from these behaviors by doing the next step. The second step is that we must detect and maximize the positive aspects of our identifications. We must have a target list for our ideal self. Who do you want to be? What do you want to do differently? The first course in any practical course of self-development is to become clearly aware of the person that you would like to be. Then it requires that we learn to live in integrity with ourselves for who we are becoming. The exercise of integrity can be as simple as learning how to keep your word. The third and final step in modifying our personality is called action reinforcement. This is when we create a situation in our lives in which we can exercise courage. It may be as simple as you addressing a matter that must be addressed. As you walk into the situation, you must remind yourself that you are more than capable of effectively addressing the situation to the point of satisfaction.

The greatest difference maker in the life of a leader or any person for that matter is inside of us; it is our attitude. When we are committed to discovering and expanding our commitment to deepening our personal and professional capacities, we will disentangle internal experience from external circumstances. This will allow us to recognize that we are the creators of the experience and not victims of the circumstances. Warren Bennis once said, "leadership is the function of knowing yourself." We can develop the type of mindset or attitude that is necessary to fully become ourselves. Dr. Myles Munroe informs us that "leadership is not a technique, a style or the acquisition of skills, but it is a demonstration of an attitude." "The thinking of a leader is what separates him or her from followers. There is nothing more powerful as attitude. Attitude dictates your response to the present and determines the quality of your future. Your attitude is a manifestation of who you think that you are." (**6**)

There are several key aspects within a person's attitude. Your attitude or mindset reveals your self-identity or who or what you identify as your source for life. Your attitude exposes your self-esteem or how much value you believe that you have as a person or a leader for our discussion. Your attitude will ultimately determine whether or not you will ever connect with your potential, those latent, dormant abilities that are inside of you. To maximize our potential, we must learn to develop our attitudes because our attitudes "determine our interpretation of and response to our environments." (**7**)

CHAPTER SEVEN: REFLECTIONS

We can learn to develop our emotions and our thoughts when we learn to mobilize our total spiritual, mental and physical resources for any endeavor that we believe in.

If we are to be the most effective in our leadership, we must develop a winner's mindset which can surmount great obstacles. In this mindset, we can learn to re-create the same state of mind at will.

It must not be beyond the leader or emerging leader to study the basic components of their minds and behaviors and how these work in concert with each other.

All winners have at least one thing in common: an ability to concentrate their attention on a single focus for a long time.

The greatest difference maker in the life of a leader or any person for that matter is inside of us; it is our attitude.

The thinking of a leader is what separates him or her from followers.

There is nothing more powerful as attitude.

Leadership from the Heart

"Not all of us can do great things but we can all do small things with great love."

Mother Teresa

It is believed that many have the calling to be a leader, but even fewer seem to have the heart to be a leader. A leadership heart is directly connected to a person's passion. However, even though a person may have a passion to lead on some level the heart to effectively lead must still be developed. The Bible has many things to say about the heart. One of the things that Jesus Christ said is, "For where your treasure is, there your heart will be also" – (Matthew 6:21 New International Version). This statement is telling us that what we value will be what we focus on. If as a leader my title, position or my brand is what I value the most, then I will focus on that. If on the other hand, I as a priority value people and their development, that will be the focus of my heart. As mentioned in the previous chapter, the heart is "the seat of the feelings, desires, affections, and aversions."

Our hearts are the decision-making centers where all of our choices are made. It is both the conscious and subconscious mind. It is also the place of understanding and reasoning. The French philosopher Blaise Paschal said, "the heart has reasons the mind knows not of...." The heart is the deepest psychological ground of our personality.

As the seat of reasoning, our hearts are also the storehouse of all of our thoughts. It is the soil for our ideas and the center of our decision making. It is the 'hard drive,' for our conscious mind. Our hearts are what motivate us in our attitudes and actions, even though we may not be aware of what is influencing it. We generally find out what is in our hearts when we are facing some type of pressure in our lives. This is when our ingrained attitudes and beliefs emerge.

Dr. Myles Munroe gave us a list of specific components that go into making up our heart attitudes and behaviors. He says:

1. What you believe about yourself comes from where you get your information.

2. What you believe comes from the way that you think.

3. Whatever you believe you are going to be that is what you will be.

4. When you change your thinking, you change what you believe. When you change your beliefs, you change your expectations. When you change your expectations you change your attitude. When you change your attitude you change your behavior.

5. If you change your behavior you change your life.

6. You will become what you have been conditioned to think that you will become.

"Your heart is the seat of your beliefs. It is the center of your philosophy, the container of the ideas that you have accepted as truth. It stores all of your ideas, beliefs, convictions, philosophies, experiences, memories, and personal thoughts. Therefore, true leadership begins with and demands a constant monitoring of what goes into our hearts." (1)

As we live out the principle of leading from the heart, one of the primary focuses that leaders must commit to is to bring out the best in others. However, successful leaders go even further; they form lasting emotional bonds. They hold people and not just projects in their hearts.

What would cause a person to hold another person in their hearts? I believe that it would be one word - love! Mahatma Gandhi said, "the day the power of love overrules the love of power, the world will know peace." This concept is the beginning of learning to lead from the heart. How do we better understand the role of leaders loving people? We must first recognize that we as human beings have been wired by God to give and receive love. I believe that we have yet to fully realize what a limitless capacity we have to further open our hearts to be more devoted to loving others.

A person cannot love another person beyond the level of love they have for themselves. It is a universal principle articulated by Jesus Christ. He said "love your neighbor as yourself." In the context of personal leadership, a person develops a natural love for others because they understand that they are essentially the same as others. True, authentic and genuine love is an amplification of the sense of yourself that empowers a person to share in the joys of others. It is finding success in the success of others. This type of thinking will encourage us to assist in the development of people.

PERSONAL LEADERSHIP LESSON

I have learned that leadership is a function, but, being a leader is a responsibility. It is a responsibility to the development and welfare of people. Whenever the function becomes more important than the responsibility it can lead to the misuse of our leadership position.

"Perhaps one of the missing ingredients in leadership today is the primary focus on results and performance more than on values such as love, care, compassion, dignity and kindness. Only an authentic, caring person can evoke a similar response from others." (2) Love is best seen in how we care for others. Yes, we can love people emotionally however loving people because we choose to love them is love in action. Love is participatory. Therefore, if we care, really care then we will provide the proper tools and training for those we are leading, enabling them to be prepared for the tasks they will perform. We will also assist them in identifying their personal gifts and strengths with the best jobs for them. We will give them active encouragement, opportunity and assistance to develop their potential for personal growth and to advance in their chosen fields of endeavors. When we really care we will not allow the personal interests and needs of people that follow our leadership to be sacrificed for the goals and intentions of others.

Without love, our responsibilities can feel like burdens that we have to bear on our shoulders every day. However, with love, we experience an inborn surge of energy, a natural desire to do the right thing, and a willing spirit of sacrifice. What has required a lot of effort becomes effortless. We will not fully understand our capacity to love until we find ourselves in situations that may call for the depths of love from our hearts. Jesus Christ consistently stressed the highest ideals in a human being so that humanity may practice peace and reconciliation. This was because of his love for people. Are there specific barriers and obstacles that we face that may hinder us from giving from the heart? Professor Hitendra Wadhwa gives us a list of potential opportunities to overcome the barriers to our learning to lead from the heart. They are as follows:

1. Mindfulness: we must learn to be fully present when we interact with others.

2. Understand their context: we need to remind ourselves of what has been happening in the other person's life since we last interacted with them. Are there certain questions we can ask them to connect with them?

3. Affirmations: we can train ourselves to practice certain affirmations like, "this is the most important person to me at the moment." "There is something interesting about this person and I am going to discover it." "Before I depart I want to leave this person with warmth and goodwill."

4. Role Models: are there people you can identify that do these things?

5. Body Language: we must be aware of our tone of voice; eye contact; touch; and smiling.

6. What if this were the last time you were to see this person? How would you like to leave them?

7. Identify something that you appreciate about the person.

8. How do you treat them when you have limited time to either have a discussion or meeting with the person?

As leaders, how do we cultivate love in everything that we do? Can love be measured? Yes, it can. It is measured as we develop our character, master our emotions and conquer adversity. The human heart has been wired to be connected. We enter this life through a connection called our parents. This human connection continues throughout our lives in one form or another. What we learn is that leading with love is attainable, but it is a step-by-step journey. The basic principle is that there is always something we can do to bring us to our ideal self. And so if our ideal self is someone who is more loving than we are today – more compassionate, caring, empathetic, forgiving, generous or selfless – know that we can get there. We simply need to find the right techniques and then start practicing them.

There are two basic keys that I believe will unlock our hearts in our everyday life. The first key recognizes that it is much easier to love someone when there is something that you appreciate about them.

However, how do we do that with people who behave in ways we don't like or respect? If we create the conditions of positive exchange and connection, it brings out the best in the other person. We are able to do that by recognizing that love is ultimately self-less, universal, unconditional and thoughtful. It will require sacrifice that may at times appear to be extreme or extraordinary. The second key makes us stand up and pay attention to our everyday interactions with people. Are you willing to learn to give one hundred percent of yourself more consistently so that it will benefit you and the other person? Why don't we give one hundred percent of ourselves regularly? Giving one hundred percent of ourselves to others more consistently does not necessarily mean pouring all of your time and energy into a person in the same way that they may be seeking it from you. It may mean that we choose to interact with them in a manner that will ultimately be beneficial to their growth.

If we think about it, what would life be without love? The greatest highs we have experienced in life are usually associated with moments when we felt a deep sense of love for someone or something. When we give of ourselves to others purely to make them happy and successful (with no interest or expectation in getting anything back), we will find a fulfillment like no other. True love will cause us to forget our own protective behaviors in the service of the higher nature of God's love that lives in us. We will identify less with our name or identity or physical form and more with the people and causes that we serve. We are not invited to ignore the misdeeds or shortcomings in others – instead we are being invited to "clear our hearts," to re-establish a calm and positive environment within ourselves so that we can think and act with a clear mind and with the aspiration of giving unconditional respect to the other person even as we pursue the causes we believe to be in the best interest of a given situation. When we feel angry, frustrated, cynical, critical or dismissive about someone this could be in the midst of an interaction with them or just as a thought that comes to us – we must activate the nature of love by engaging in controlling what we choose to think about them in that instance.

Dr. Martin Luther King, Jr. said, "everybody can be great because everybody can serve. You don't have to make your subject and verb agree to serve. You only need a heart full of grace, a soul generated by love." As we tune into someone else's experience we can recognize the love we already practice in our lives. Many great leaders have been transformative leaders because they loved people.

CHAPTER EIGHT: REFLECTIONS

It is believed that many have the calling to be a leader, but fewer seem to have the heart for it.

Our hearts are the decision-making center where all of our choices are made. It is both the conscious and subconscious mind.

Your heart is the seat of your beliefs. It is the center of your philosophy, the container of the ideas that you have accepted as truth. It stores all of your ideas, beliefs, convictions, philosophies, experiences, memories, and personal thoughts.

Perhaps one of the missing ingredients in leadership today is the primary focus on results and performance more than on values such as love, care, compassion, dignity and kindness. Only an authentic, caring person can evoke a similar response from others.

We will not fully understand our capacity to love until we find ourselves in situations that may call for the depths of love from our hearts.

Can love be measured? Yes, it can.

PART TWO

PEOPLE LEADERSHIP

Becoming the Leader that You Would Follow

"The most powerful leadership tool you have is your own personal example."

John Wooden

I would like to begin this part of our discussion with this question. What have been the most important qualities that you have looked for in the leaders that have been in your life?

One leadership study indicated that the most important quality that many people look for and admire in a leader is personal credibility. Credibility is a mosaic stone in the leadership foundation. If we don't believe in the messenger, we will not believe the message. Authentic leadership is the place where the person does not just perform the message but becomes the message.

According to the dictionary, credibility is defined as "the quality of being believable or worthy of trust." Credibility is reinforced by integrity. A person of integrity is a person of principle. A person of integrity is a person who has learned or is learning to live from the core of their being. A person of integrity is given more to being and not just doing. They don't usually get to this point in their lives without overcoming several different obstacles. In spite of any obstacle, they have chosen to become a person that earns the trust of others. They are people who 'practice what they preach…"put their money where their mouth is…"walk the talk…"have actions that speak louder than their words…"have the courage to live their convictions." Enclosed in these everyday expressions are two of the essential qualities necessary for earning and sustaining personal credibility. First, leaders must be clear about their beliefs. They must know what they stand for and then put what they say into practice. In other words, they must act on their beliefs.

Since leaders generally represent groups of people, when they speak and act, they are generally doing so on behalf of others. Personal credibility is built and maintained when a person does what they say. The commitment to being or becoming a credible leader begins with the clarification of a person's values, visions and passions. It is difficult to do what you say until you have clarity about what you want to say. Therefore, what a leader says must become something that a leader has committed himself or herself to live out in their own lives. A leader must actually care about what they say they believe. Their leadership cannot only be a theory it must become a practice. According to Jim Kouzes, a leader must ask the following questions to learn how to build the type of credibility it takes to be an effective leader:

- What are the values and principles that guide you?

- What do you care about?

- What keeps you up at night?

- What legacy do you want to leave?

- What's your framework for living?

Once a leader can clearly articulate the values and beliefs that they live by, they have taken the first step towards building sustainable credibility. However, this is only the first step. If a leader is standing on specific principles in their leadership they will still be required to execute the fulfillment of those principles in their responsibilities. Having a set of guiding values is of the utmost importance, but values alone will not cause a person to be an effective leader. You must not only be able to do what you say, but also learn how to do what you say well. This involves being aware of your strengths and weaknesses. It also involves being committed to gathering and processing useful information concerning the development of your leadership skills and abilities. Some people call the development of these skills and abilities, leadership competencies. In their book, The Leadership Challenge authors Jim Kouzes and Barry Posner outline five practices of exemplary leaders. These five qualities are engaged by leaders when they are operating at their best, when they are being or becoming the leaders that they themselves would follow.

The first practice is <u>Modeling the Way</u>. According to Kouzes and Posner, "leaders find their voice by clarifying their personal values and then expressing those values in their own style. Then they set the example by aligning their personal actions with shared values." (**1**)

The second practice is <u>Inspiring a Shared Vision</u>. "Leaders envision the future by imagining exciting and ennobling possibilities, and they enlist others in their dreams by appealing to shared aspirations." (**2**)

The third practice is <u>Challenging the Process</u>. "Leaders search for opportunities by seeking innovative ways to change, grow and improve. Leaders also experiment and take risks by constantly generating small victories and learning from mistakes." (**3**)

The fourth practice is <u>Enabling Others to Act</u>. "Leaders foster collaboration by promoting cooperative goals and building trust. They strengthen others by sharing power and discretion." (**4**)

The fifth practice is <u>Encouraging the Heart</u>. "To keep hope and determination alive, leaders recognize the contributions of others by showing appreciation for individual excellence. They also celebrate the values and the victories by creating a spirit of community." (**5**)

PEOPLE LEADERSHIP LESSON

My experiences in leadership have taught me that credibility is earned and should not be expected until it is earned. This earning is not proving anything; it is releasing from within the qualities of our inherent leadership spirit.

Throughout the years, I have had the privilege of working with many wonderful leaders. Upon reflection, the best of the best have two qualities in common. They love people and are passionate about leading. Their approach generally reveals this about them. As Frances Hesselbein states, "leadership is "circular," with the leader reaching across the organization to colleagues, not down to subordinates."

A leader who understands that leadership is not just about the leader is one whom others desire to follow. Leadership is more about the great people that they are working with. What often happens is that because some leaders are charismatic, naturally gifted or have developed their gifts to the point of being productive, they receive a certain status. There is nothing inherently wrong with this status; it only becomes dangerous when that status is accentuated and reinforced in damaging demonstrations of power on those under that leader's leadership. However, in the truest essence of leadership, a leader whom others would follow understands that their leadership is ultimately determined by whether or not people give them the privilege of their followership.

Jesus Christ handled the issue of status in leadership by the gathering his key followers together one day and washing their dusty feet. Then he said to them, "do as I have done to you." (John 13:15 New Living Translation). Jesus Christ has been physically removed from this plane of existence for the past one thousand nine hundred and eighty-three years, yet his organization still has more than half of the people living on this planet as His followers. It has grown exponentially and influences the belief systems of entire nations and people groups. "Leadership is a special function but it really carries no status with it whatsoever." It actually doesn't carry status because it is not ultimately for the benefit of the leader rather it is for the development of people. Leaders can and should be recognized or acknowledged for their contributions however, when leadership separates leaders from the common ground of their own humanity and places a person as superior and another inferior I believe that it leads to a lost perspective on who or what a leader really is.

I believe that assessment of a leader's potential for being the type of leader that you or I would follow begins with the question "How much do you love people?" Even though some high levels of leadership bring status, power or money, these benefits come at a cost. Almost all great leaders work extremely hard, take their jobs very personally, are subject too ongoing (and sometimes unfair) criticism and pay a price for their achievements. Yet because of their love for people and love of leading people they consider these situations opportunities for learning and understanding. A leader can only inspire the people that they are leading if they are themselves inspired to lead.

There are other qualities that I believe to be crucial to becoming the type of leader that you would follow:

1. Productive leaders learn to listen beyond the words that they hear others speak. There is no substitute for learning how to really listen on a deep level. This is so that you can be clear about what you have heard from people. This can be accomplished in many different ways; however, asking questions is one of my favorite ways of really listening.

2. Productive leaders have the courage to live their convictions. You have to be willing to say the unpopular, unpleasant thing if it is the truth. This means not only telling others the truth but also telling yourself the truth.

3. Productive leaders have to fight against their own arrogance. After a period of time, it becomes easier to think that you know what needs to be known about leadership and leadership development. This is not to say that you don't have experience; however, if we ever stop learning, we become unproductive.

4. Productive leaders are flexible. Each of us can point to time-tested methods that have worked for us as leaders. We know they work. Yet in the climate of constant change that we are living in, we have to at least be willing to look at different methods to getting things accomplished. Of course there can be risk in being flexible, yet a leader understands that his or her way of doing things may not always be the best for those that they are leading.

5. Productive leaders learn when to talk and when to be quiet. When we talk, we must be willing to stand behind what we say and do what we say we are going to do. This also includes knowing when to keep in confidence things that are spoken to us by others.

6. Productive leaders know when to say no. It is very tempting to say yes to everything, but it is not realistic. I have come to find that people can appreciate it more when you are not able to do something and you say so. Your credibility will increase when people know that your yes means yes and your no means no.

7. Productive leaders understand that people are individuals even though they are a part of the team. Sometimes when you are under pressure as a leader, you can forget that people have varying interests, abilities, goals and styles of learning. Therefore, it is important to understand what makes each person function the way that they function so you can customize your interactions with them.

8. Productive leaders are big on meaning and articulating a clear purpose. The reason that some people don't understand what their leaders are communicating to them is not necessarily in the strategy. It is probably not the intelligence of the person. It is generally because they don't understand the meaning of what is being communicated. The "why" question has to be answered. When people solve a problem or understand the why, it gives them more meaning in what they are involved with.

9. Productive leaders focus on feedback. Feedback must be clear, honest and constructive. A well-orchestrated team depends on everyone doing their job, at the time they are supposed to do it, yielding the results they are supposed to yield. This is why we need consequences; they remind us that not keeping our commitments will carry repercussions.

10. Productive leaders learn to be resourceful. Be open to new ideas in your leadership style, vision, expectations, and feedback. If change becomes necessary, acknowledge it quickly. Asking for feedback is a very powerful tool, one that can be successfully used to maximize engagement and growth. Just make sure you also plan and invest resources in the follow up. The damage happens when a leader asks for feedback and then either does nothing to improve himself or herself or attempts to identify the source of criticism and punish it. Persecuting someone who took a risk to respond to your request is an obvious trust breaker.

CHAPTER NINE: REFLECTIONS

One leadership study indicated that the most important quality that many people look for and admire in a leader is personal credibility.

Authentic leadership is the place where the person does not just perform the message but becomes the message.

Personal credibility is built and maintained when a person does what they say.

Having a set of guiding values is of the utmost importance however, values alone will not cause a person to be an effective leader. You must not only be able to do what you say but also learn how to do what you say well.

Leadership is "circular," with the leader reaching across the organization to colleagues, not down to subordinates.

The Greatest Good of Leadership

"The role of leaders is not to get other people to follow them but to empower others to lead."

Bill George

A new science of leadership has emerged and the emphasis appears to be on the fundamental nature of leadership. That fundamental nature is empowerment. Empowerment is an often used term that we hear a lot about in leadership today. Empowerment is defined as "the giving or delegation of power or authority; authorization; the giving of an ability; enablement or permission". Empowerment is based on the belief that people have the ability – and want to take on more responsibility. Empowerment is also based on the premise that people have God-given potential that must be cultivated, nurtured and released. Empowerment is a way to give people greater authority and responsibility for making influential decisions. Joseph Juran defined empowerment as "conferring the right to make decisions and take action."

Empowerment is predicated on trust. When a leader trusts the people and processes that they are engaged in, they can freely empower others to participate. If that same leader doesn't trust people or processes, they will generally resort to using control or manipulation as a dominant leadership practice. Often, this type of response is not always the result of what others have done to a leader; rather, it is an expression of how those leaders think about themselves and their leadership. When this takes place, people are viewed as limitations and barriers as opposed to gifts from God. Since leaders are inclined to figure out situations before anyone else, they have the capacity to take advantage of others. For this reason, it is essential to regularly question your motives. There is a fine line between manipulation and motivation. The first moves people for personal benefit, while the latter moves people for mutual gain.

The authenticity of a leader's leadership is found in the ability to empower others. This is the sacrificial nature of leadership, whether you are a parent or the head of a Fortune 500 company. Empowering others is the ethic from which many influential and impactful leaders have lived their lives. The one I consider to be the greatest of all of them is Jesus Christ. His lifestyle was one of sacrifice and empowerment. His empowerment was first and foremost based upon knowing whom He was called to lead and in what way He was called to serve them. He was willing to give His life to this cause. He operated from a bottom up and not a top down paradigm. When people encountered Him, they would not leave His presence the same way in which they came to Him. At the same time, He was not detached from the human challenges that leaders face who are committed to empowering their followers. He had to endure the contradictions of people who would in one moment say that they were with Him and for Him, but in another instance wanted to see Him destroyed. He was not afraid to make the difficult decisions, even in His own life. Once He had to make a decision as to whether or not He was going to follow through with the plan that was in place for His life. He was willing to stand alone for others. There was a woman who was found in a compromising situation and He was the only one that would stand up for her. He interacted with people who were outcasts in His community. He empowered people who would have otherwise been in devastating circumstances for the remainder of their lives had He not stepped in and revealed to them their true value as humans. He refused to be impartial or show favoritism to one person or group of people over another. Possibly His greatest act of empowerment was that He was willing to represent the cause of empowering people that He came to earth to empower without being deterred.

PERSONAL LEADERSHIP LESSON

Empowerment is about possibilities. When leaders are committed to the possibilities for others, then they are in the empowerment mode. I have implemented empowerment in my interactions with emerging leaders by encouraging them to be themselves and not comparing themselves with others.

According to Steve Zaffron and Dave Logan in their book The Three Laws of Performance, "when there is a culture of leadership (empowerment), boundaries that have impeded performance in the past naturally dissolve. People report a sense of unity and collective possibility." "As John Kotter and others have pointed out, people who try to use management when leadership is called for end up suppressing innovation. Leadership, on the other hand, is about generating new futures. It involves balancing a series of complex forces. There is no one tried and true path. Every situation requires something unique to it. The leader has to take everything into account, including especially how situations occur to people." (**1**)

In his book entitled Principled-Centered Leadership, author Steven R. Covey lists five conditions of empowerment. He suggests that in order to motivate people to function at their highest levels, a leader or leaders must first find the areas where the needs and goals of the company or organization overlap individual needs, goals and capabilities. He calls this a win-win agreement. This win-win agreement is buttressed by self-supervision, building structures and systems that release the potential in people and establishing the accountability mechanisms needed to maintain understanding and commitment to a common vision.

The five conditions are as follows:

1. First, specify desired results. This means learning to discuss what results are expected. Being specific about the quantity and quality.

2. Second, set some guidelines. Communicate whatever principles, policies and procedures are considered essential to getting desired results.

3. Third, identify available resources. Identify the various financial, human, technical and organizational resources available to people to assist them in getting desired results.

4. Fourth, define accountability. Holding people accountable for results puts teeth into the win-win agreement.

5. Fifth, determine the consequences. Reach an understanding of what follows when the desired results are achieved or not achieved.

One of the primary goals of empowerment is to move people from an externally controlled life to an internally controlled life. This takes place as people are given guidance for their lives. In addition, when the necessary resources are available to the person being empowered it will assist them in establishing the standards for the improvement of their activities.

Leaders play an important role because the types of environments that are designed has a lot to do with whether people will experience being empowered. Therefore, as Steven R. Covey states, a smart leader would say, "we have to be aware of the culture of our organization or company, of the nature of the situation, of the social will."

This brings to bear the responsibility of leaders intentionally developing environments in which emerging leaders can become empowered. How can existing leaders assist in the removal of the excess structural barriers that can hinder the empowerment of people and give people the freedom and flexibility to think and act in ways that increase their leadership abilities?

How do we develop a cultures and communities of empowerment? Patricia Lotich gives us thirteen areas that are important to the design of an empowered culture. They are as follows:

1. **Existing leaders must be committed to supporting a people empowered culture.** This includes developing an organizational definition of empowerment that may include well defined boundaries and management training on how to lead emerging leaders.

2. **People empowerment is centered on the needs of the people.** When people are empowered to make decisions that help others, they are contributing to the strategy and business objectives of the organization.

3. **Established leaders hand over a level of the decision making power to emerging leaders**. This act of delegation may be something as simple as allowing a person to make a leadership decision.

4. **Emerging leaders are trained to take on new people focused responsibilities**. Training may include service, problem solving, negotiation and conflict resolution skills.

5. **Emerging leaders are given access to information and data that can be used in their decision making process**. This information might include feedback from surveys or comment cards that can help make informed people-focused decisions.

6. **Existing leaders must develop trust and confidence in emerging leaders to make the right decisions.** An existing leader who second-guesses an emerging leaders every decision can impact an emerging leader's confidence in their decision making ability.

7. **Authority and decision making responsibility come with specific expectations and boundaries.** For example, an emerging leader may be empowered to correct a situation for another person up to a certain point.

8. **Emerging leaders are provided mentors.** Mentors should be someone who has successfully done something that the emerging leader is learning to do. For example, if an emerging leader is learning to be empowered to perform a specific service, their mentor should be someone who has learned the critical thinking skills to assess different situations and come to reasonable conclusions with them.

9. **As emerging leaders develop their skills, they are provided positive reinforcement and coaching as they maneuver different decision making scenarios.** We all make mistakes when we first begin making decisions so it is important to provide good coaching and positive reinforcement.

10. **Performance expectations are aligned around organizational needs.** This will reinforce an emerging leader's motivation to make the right decisions.

11. **Assess social styles to match emerging leader's competencies with job responsibilities.** Using an effective assessment tool can help identify the emerging leader's strengths.

12. **Emerging leaders are provided the appropriate tools and equipment to do their job**. Some emerging leaders are very vocal about their needs, but others will work with aging equipment and never speak up. Assessing changing technology and equipment should be part of an organization's strategy for empowering emerging leaders.

13. **Have a plan to implement an empowerment environment**. Implementation should be mapped out and a timeline for all aspects should be written so all understand the timing and process of implementation.

Organizations with strong empowerment models show that productivity improves within an empowered culture. President Theodore Roosevelt said "the best executive is the one who has sense enough to pick good men to do what he wants done, and self-restraint enough to keep from meddling with them while they do it."

The empowerment of emerging leaders is similar to getting players of a team into the game to play the game. Practice is important, but the real action is on the court in the field of play. The goal of empowerment is the release of the potential of all of the players on the team.

"A clear model of leadership empowerment provides direct access to the actual nature of being when one is 'on the court', real-time, being a leader, and opens up and reveals the source of one's actions when one is 'on the court', real-time, exercising leadership." **(2)** This methodology when used provides direct access to where the real action is taking place which in 'on the court.'

CHAPTER TEN: REFLECTIONS

The fundamental nature of leadership is empowerment.

The authenticity of a leader's leadership is found in the ability to empower others.

When there is a culture of leadership (empowerment), boundaries that have impeded performance in the past naturally dissolve.

One of the primary goals of empowerment is to move people from an externally controlled life to an internally controlled life.

The Leader as Coach and Mentor

"The only real training for leadership is leadership."

A. Jay

Historically, the concept of coaching in business has primarily concentrated on the performance issues of key leaders in a company or organization. Generally, those performance issues were considered potentially detrimental to the company or organization. However, the leader or leaders that were intended to receive the coaching were either valuable people to the company or organization or their removal may have precipitated too much change at one time. Today, coaching has taken on a different connotation which doesn't necessarily mean that a person begins with the idea of solving a problem. The marketplace has become increasingly competitive and fast-moving which has caused companies and organizations to recognize that they must enable key people to achieve critical business objectives. This is often accomplished through coaching.

In addition, today because of the conscious effort of individuals committed to personal growth and development, a number of people utilize what are called life coaches or personal coaches. Coaching has embraced an entirely new focus which is "how to take good people and make them the best that they can be."

"Coaching is an approach, a viewpoint, and a technique as much as it is a profession. There are no defined backgrounds or skill sets for coaches, just as there are no defined sets of problems or challenges. The coach is a highly specific resource of knowledge, expertise, intuition and experience. He or she brings to the table the ability to deal with dynamic challenges." (1)

Mentoring has been much less understood than coaching in my opinion, and probably even much less utilized. Therefore, what connection do mentoring and coaching have to each other? One of the better definitions that I have heard for mentoring comes from J. Robert Clinton, he says, "mentoring refers to the process where a person with a serving, giving, encouraging attitude, the mentor, sees leadership potential in a still-to-be developed person, the protégé, and is able to promote or otherwise significantly influence the protégé along in the realization of potential." (2) Clinton said, "a mentor is someone who helps a protégé in some very practical ways: by giving timely advice that encourages the protégé; by risking his or her own reputation in backing the protégé; by bridging between the protégé and needed resources; by modeling and setting expectations that challenge the protégé; by giving tracts, letters, books or other literary information that open perspectives for the protégé; by giving financially, sometimes sacrificially, to further the protégé's ministry (work); by co-ministering (cooperating) in order to increase the credibility, status, and prestige of the protégé; and by having the freedom to allow and even promote the protégé beyond the mentor's own level of leadership." (3)

While coaching and mentoring have a number of similarities, coaching tends to be centered on performance development and mentoring appears to be centered on character development or the embodiment of specific ideas. Coaching is often by its nature "a flexible, adaptable and fluid way of achieving measurable results." (4) Mentoring is often by its nature a "flexible and patient process, that recognizes that it takes time and experience for a person to develop." (5) This is the being and doing dynamic that is necessary to a person becoming an effective leader. Therefore, for the purposes of our discussion I will focus on mentoring as the development of being and coaching as the development for doing.

Coaching

In the discussion about coaching, not everyone is talking about the same thing when they use that term. In this discussion, coaching is based upon the idea of coaching for leadership development. Coaching for leadership development generally has a beginning and an ending. The parameters are usually established for what the expected outcomes are going to be from the interaction. The criteria for coaches when coaching is as Frances Hesselbein has said must be, "first do no harm."

I believe a coach's priority must be to assist people in seeing, thinking and communicating from a perspective of what is possible. This requires courage, specifically, the courage "to see reality as it actually is – to collude against illusion." (6) It also requires the courage to imagine something better than what is currently being displayed. Then it requires the courage to "communicate reality and possibility so powerfully that others can't help but move forward towards a better future." (7)

Coaching generally focuses the attention on the person or person's being coached in general areas. Those areas can be specified as time goes on to address the specific roles that each person will engage. However, a coach wants to first make sure that there is a general awareness of what is being focused on. When that happens, the coach will want to know that each person is committed to the same goals. This is achieved by each person having the information and training that is necessary for them to fulfill their specific responsibilities in an effective manner. Then, as people are gathered together around specific goals or objectives, the vision for what is expected to reach those goals can then be communicated in a clear fashion. These first two steps lead to the third primary step. This is to put into action what the person is committed to learning and understanding. These are called actionable objectives. As people who are being coached begin to implement the techniques that they have received, then the alignment of the individuals and the team's objectives can begin to take place. There will be changes necessary when attempting to shift thoughts and behaviors in people and organizations. The final coaching component in this scenario is measuring whether the evaluative tools that are used to assess whether or not things are on course or if what was desired has taken place are then implemented.

When you are a coach, you must know your material. Know and be fully committed to the principles that you profess. You have to declare your expectations and show uncommon commitment to the welfare of those that you are coaching. Undeclared expectations are not fair to others. People should not be expected to be able to read the minds of their leaders. We must also be committed to the implementation of the plans that are developed from those expectations. A coach also generally has positive expectations and is able to effectively communicate this. These positive expectations can be maintained through enthusiasm. Coaches take care of the people that they are connected to, which means that you make them a priority. Then coaches must recognize that there are those occasions where they will have to personally demonstrate what it is that they are communicating. The essence of leadership is going out in front and showing the way. This is also the essence of coaching.

One of the primary goals of coaching is talent development. It is the evolution of several different types of contributory factors that can become strategies that can assist the person coaching. For instance, some of the important skills that are needed to be an effective coach include learning how to communicate often and connect team members to critical information. Research shows that engagement is the highest when coaches and those that they are coaching communicate regularly, whether by phone, digitally or face-to-face. The documentation of processes and outcomes is another necessary skill. The documentation is critical for identifying milestones or changes that take place. It is also important for a coach to exhibit a learning mind-set. Continuous change means needing to learn and adapt. A part of this comes from embracing learning as the coach and encouraging others to push beyond their comfort zones. The role of a coach is not to micromanage, but to coach the person or the team to the right answers. Coaches must learn to develop people and teams from solutions providers to architects of sustained growth. This growth must shift from managing processes to driving outcomes that can create a significant impact within an organization. This can take place when a coach understands the social aspects of leadership development. The primary social aspect of leadership development keeps people at the core of its activities. It designs capabilities and culture by enabling each person to reach their fullest potential in environments of empowerment.

Mentoring

Someone once said, "adversity does not build character, it reveals it." This is where mentoring becomes important in the development of an emerging leader. "Almost every case study indicates that one major key to an emerging leader's development involves significant people who come along their path at crucial times. These individuals were usually further along in their leadership pilgrimage and from that vantage point are able to encourage the emerging leader in their development in numerous ways. The common thread in all of these encounters was that of a relational experience which empowered (developed, enabled, provided needed resources) the emerging leader in some needed way at that time. This notion of God ordained relationships is at the heart of the mentoring concept. Mentoring can be both a low accountability process or a high accountability process depending on the deliberateness or accountability involved. Mentoring is at its core a relational process, in which someone who knows or understands something, (the mentor), then transfers that something (the power resources), to someone else, (the mentee), at a sensitive time so that it impacts the development of that person."

PERSONAL LEADERSHIP LESSON

I believe that mentors often need mentors too. A mistake that I have discovered in my own leadership is that when you as a leader believe that you either don't need or cannot be mentored, you will stunt your own development. I am constantly learning to ask myself what it is that I can learn from other leaders?

Mentoring is ultimately an agreement between a mentor and a mentee. When a mentor finds someone that they believe that they can personally mentor, they need to have a set of guidelines or expectations that they develop. This is also true for the mentee. Mentoring is not only an agreement; it must also be intentional to derive the greatest benefit for both the mentor and mentee.

According to Myles Munroe in his book entitled, "Passing It On," there are a set of specific concepts that a mentor and mentee can incorporate into their relationship for it to become a productive process for both. I consider these agreements that the mentor makes with themselves before embarking upon the journey of mentoring others. They are:

"**I agree to mentor** – as a mentor, you must be willing to consider and accept the commitment, cost and dedication required to mentor.

I understand that leadership is "caught" more than taught – as a mentor, you must acknowledge that successful mentoring demands in an interactive relationship with your mentee, providing opportunities to observe, listen, ask questions, understudy, and learn in your environment.

I will see potential in each person I mentor – as a mentor, you must see the hidden treasure within the mentee and be motivated by what he/she could become and not judge them on what they are now.

I will tolerate mistakes – as a mentor, you must be willing to make room for the learning process of the mentee, being ever mindful that you are also a product of many failures and mistakes, which were all a part of the development process.

I will demonstrate patience – as a mentor, you must cultivate a high tolerance level for the developmental process of the mentee and enlarge your capacity to handle the missteps of your mentee.

I will make time to spend with the mentee – as a mentor, you must be willing to invest your time in and share physical space with the mentee, as well as to accept that mentoring will demand time and effort from you.

I will provide opportunities to learn - as a mentor, you must be willing to create or invite the mentee to share your platform and exposure in different environments and situations for the purpose of personal development and training.

I will be honest with correction and generous with praise – as a mentor, you must be willing to confront the mentee on issues when necessary and not miss any opportunity to convert negative situations into teaching moments. You must also encourage and motivate the mentee with affirmations and also praise your protégé when appropriate.

I will provide recognition – as a mentor, you must be willing to recognize the value of the mentee and share that value with others in your sphere of influence.

I will focus on managing things and developing people – as a mentor, you must be willing to always place the human factor above material or mechanical things. Human development will be your principle motivation.

I understand that transformation comes only through association – as a mentor, you must accept responsibility for transferring your knowledge, wisdom, resources, relationships and opportunities to your mentee through a close relationship with you.

I will view people as opportunities, not interruptions – as a mentor, you must be willing to allow the mentee to enter your personal space when appropriate and always make yourself accessible. The mentee should never feel that he or she is a burden or interference in your life.

I will have a long-term perspective – as a mentor, you must always be aware that the purpose and goal of mentoring is the future. Maintaining a comprehensive view of the bigger picture is mandatory." (**8**)

"Mentorship requires an explicit understanding between two parties. It demands commitment, dedication, submission, responsibility and accountability." (**9**)

CHAPTER ELEVEN: REFLECTIONS

Coaching is an approach, a viewpoint, and a technique as much as it is a profession. There are no defined backgrounds or skill sets for coaches, just as there are no defined sets of problems or challenges.

Mentoring refers to the process where a person with a serving, giving, encouraging attitude, the mentor, sees leadership potential in a still-to-be developed person, the protégé, and is able to promote or otherwise significantly influence the protégé along in the realization of potential.

While coaching and mentoring have a number of similarities coaching tends to be centered on performance development and mentoring appears to be centered on character development or the embodiment of specific ideas.

Coaching generally focuses the attention on the person or person's being coached on general areas.

Mentoring is at its core a relational process, in which someone who knows or understands something, (the mentor), then transfers that something (the power resources), to someone else, (the mentee), at a sensitive time so that it impacts the development of that person.

Leadership Training and Leadership Development

"Before you are a leader, success is all about growing yourself. When you become a leader, success is all about growing others."

Jack Welch

In the discussion, I want to acknowledge that there is a distinct difference between training and development. At a certain point in my development, I understood them to be the same and they are not. Unfortunately, many people confuse leadership development and leadership training. This is a mistake because training is only a part of leadership development, not the entire process. Leadership development is a comprehensive process that consists of the identification of potential leaders; training of potential leaders; providing support for potential leaders in the form of mentorship and ongoing training; integrating potential leaders into the decision making process; integrating potential leaders into the management team; and identifying the next group of potential leaders. Development is about connecting to a broader context than just our individual assignments.

The best way to begin a leadership development effort is to identify the characteristics that are needed for potential leaders. After that, start examining the leadership context to see who has those characteristics. These characteristics can include character traits such as vision, wisdom, decision making, a positive attitude, courage, strength, honesty, humility, high energy, integrity, responsibility, a good self-image, loyalty, emotional intelligence, honor etc. It can also include specific skills, knowledge and expertise. For example, it can include but not be limited to an understanding of the vision of the organization or company, a familiarity with the business or familiarity with a new technology. Sitting down and writing out a list of these qualities is a good first step in a leadership development process. Once this is done, you can assess the team or the emerging leader to see if you think somebody has these characteristics. Another good means of doing this is asking who could be a potential leader. Be careful not to confuse popularity with leadership when you do this. A person who is well liked would not necessarily be a good leader. Many people who are competent in other fields do not always make effective leaders particularly if they have not been developed. On the other hand, there is the possibility that, that same person does have the leadership competencies necessary to be an effective leader. A number of people may have a clear understanding of management but this doesn't necessarily mean that they are capable leaders. Once the individuals have been identified, you can launch a leadership development process. The process will probably take several months and involve several levels of work. It is always a good idea to have a selection of candidates because not every candidate will work out.

Definition of Training

Training is a process in which the emerging leader gets an opportunity to learn the key skills required to do the job. Learning with earning is known as training. It helps the person to know the complete job requirements.

Today, many organizations organize a training program for the new participants just after their selection and induction, to let them know about the rules, policies and procedures for directing their behavior and attitude as per the organizational needs. Training also helps emerging leaders to change their conduct towards their superior, subordinates and colleagues. It helps to groom them for their prospective responsibilities.

Induction training, apprenticeship training, job training, promotional training and internship training are some of the major types of training. The merits of the training are as follows:

- It can result in higher productivity both quantitatively and qualitatively.

- It develops a number of skills in the emerging leaders.

- Improved performances.

- It can create a cooperative environment in the organization.

- It builds confidence in the leadership team for doing a job.

- Decreases leadership turnover.

- It lessens the chances of miscalculations.

PEOPLE LEADERSHIP LESSON

The means to maximizing your training is the development of both "skill" and "discipline". I have found that leaders understand that growth comes from risk and pressure: "no pain-no gain." Leaders also understand that responsibility produces ownership of your training processes. Leaders understand that the fastest way to learn is to teach, which is where your true development takes place.

Definition of Development

The training for the purposes of building a sustainable leadership ethos is considered development, or executive development. It is a systematic on-going procedure in which a leader or an emerging leader learns to enhance their conceptual knowledge. It helps the individual to bring efficiency and effectiveness to their work performances.

Development is not only limited to a specific task, but it aims to improve their personality and attitude for their comprehensive growth which will help them to face future challenges. It changes the mindset of the leader and emerging leader and helps them to be equipped with a higher level of competency for leadership.

As technology needs updating, manpower in the organization also needs to be updated; development is a must. Development is an unending educational process, as education has no visible end. It involves training a person for broader assignments. It identifies and enhances the talents of the person and helps them in the application of the new knowledge they have received.

The performance of an organization is based on the quality of the leaders who are a part of it. The greater the quality of leadership development, the greater the potential will be for effective performance. The main purpose of development is to keep an unending flow of leaders or emerging leaders who are prepared for future replacement of existing leaders in an organization. This type of thinking also gives existing leaders the opportunity to explore their development in new areas.

Below is a list of twenty of the main differences between training and development:

1. Training focuses on what is normal – Development focuses on what is beyond the norm.

2. Training focuses on technique/content/curriculum – Development focuses on people.

3. Training tests patience – Development tests courage.

4. Training focuses on the present – Development focuses on the future.

5. Training adheres to standards – Development focuses on maximizing potential.

6. Training is transactional – Development is transformational.

7. Training focuses on maintenance – Development focuses on growth.

8. Training focuses on the role – Development focuses on the person.

9. Training indoctrinates – Development educates.

10. Training maintains the status quo – Development catalyzes innovation.

11. Training stifles culture – Development enriches culture.

12. Training encourages compliance – Development emphasizes performance.

13. Training focuses on efficiency – Development focuses on effectiveness.

14. Training focuses on problems - Development focuses on solutions.

15. Training focuses on reporting – Development expands influence.

16. Training places people in a box – Development frees them from the box.

17. Training is mechanical – Development is intellectual.

18. Training focuses on the known – Development explores the unknown.

19. Training places people in a comfort zone – Development moves people beyond their comfort zones.

20. Training is finite – Development is infinite.

"If what you desire is a robotic, static thinker – train them. If you're seeking innovative, critical thinkers – develop them. It is impossible to have an enterprise which is growing and evolving if the leadership is not."

The Purpose of Training in the simplest terms is:

To provide the ability to undertake a task or job...

To improve productivity and workforce flexibility...

To improve safety and quality...

To develop the capability of the workforce...

The Purpose of Development in the simplest terms is:

More productive leadership that comes from better educated and informed leaders and emerging leaders. Research has shown that the performance of leaders can be improved through:

Increased knowledge...

Changing attitudes...

Increased capability and skills...

The purpose of 'development' is to improve leadership effectiveness through planned and structured learning. A planned approach to developing leaders will enable the growth of emerging leaders. It will also provide for the future needs of the business or organization.

According to Stephen R. Covey, "all real growth and progress is made step by step, following a natural sequence of development."

This development is needed for personal improvement and it takes place in four primary areas. Those areas are personal and professional development with the aim to build trustworthiness into the character of the leader. The second area is interpersonal relations. It is through the development of consistency in our interpersonal relationships that we are able to gain the trust of others. The third area is leadership effectiveness. Leadership effectiveness begins and ends in the empowerment of others. The fourth area is organizational productivity. Increased organizational productivity leads to an aligning of the shared goals of individuals. (**1**)

"Growth and progress come by way of a sequential process. Yet many traditional paradigms of training are non-developmental. They assume that you do not really need to go through a process: you can just move in at any level and improve the situation with a quick fix. The sequential developmental process is powerfully communicated through understanding that real progress starts with self and works from the inside out." (**2**)

CHAPTER TWELVE: REFLECTIONS

Training is a process in which the emerging leader gets an opportunity to learn the key skills which are required to do the job.

Development is not only limited to a specific task, but it aims to improve their personality and attitude for their comprehensive growth which will help them to face future challenges.

The performance of an organization is based on the quality of the leaders which are a part of it and so the greater the quality of leadership development, the greater the potential will be for effective performance.

If what you desire is a robotic, static thinker – train them. If you're seeking innovative, critical thinkers – develop them. It is impossible to have an enterprise which is growing and evolving if the leadership is not.

All real growth and progress is made step by step, following a natural sequence of development.

Transforming Followers Into Leaders

"Trapped within every follower is an undiscovered leader."

Dr. Myles Munroe

The transformation of followers into leaders can begin a very extensive conversation among existing leaders. It probably depends more on how an existing leader has been conditioned to view leadership in the broadest sense of the word. This is also probably a deciding factor in determining whether or not they can see followers becoming leaders. Many historical theories about leadership can also lead one to believe that there are specific criteria for a person to become a leader. For instance, in the arena of leadership theories, some of the more popular theories are the behavioral theory, the trait theory and the contingency theory. There are of course several other leadership theories however, these are some of the more popular ones.

The behavioral theory basically believes that leadership is the designation of an elite group of people. It is usually based upon pedigree or the status. The trait theory fundamentally indicates that leaders are born and not made or developed. This of course would reinforce the behavioral theory because if a leader can only be born, it stands to reason that a person who doesn't fit that initial criteria cannot be a leader. One of the key challenges that I have with this theory is that it has never been clearly communicated who establishes the criteria to determine who is born this way. The contingency theory basically believes that leadership is a role that someone plays and not an essence. Therefore, leadership would primarily be considered a function and not a process that can assist in the development of a person's full potential.

While many of the accepted leadership theories have some merit, to be confined by them would only reinforce a paradigm that has long ago shifted. Traditional leadership logic which generally follows the leader to follower model says that organizations need a strong leader to take command and control over an organization in order for it to succeed. This model worked exceptionally well in the past when workers performed tasks that are more physical in nature, like construction or building widgets on an assembly line. However, over the past several decades, we've seen a shift from physical-labor oriented jobs to thought and connection centered work. Today's workers are not simply motivated the same way as their grandparents were. This is common knowledge, yet many insist on continuing to attempt to lead this new breed of workers as if they were still working on the factory floor.

PEOPLE LEADERSHIP LESSON

I began my leadership journey when traditional leadership theories dominated the leadership philosophy of many leaders. I didn't know it at the time that these theories existed however, when I read leadership books many of those theories were apparent. Fortunately, I have never been a person that believes that someone else can define who I am better than my Creator. Therefore, leadership theories may be a starting place for some but they should not be looked to as the final determining factor of your leadership style or abilities.

A more effective approach to leading today's thought workers is to adopt a leader to emerging leader model. In its simplest form, the leader to emerging leader model forces you to push power and responsibility as low on the organizational hierarchy as possible. This allows leaders at every level to re-focus their efforts on more meaningful tasks, while trusting those below them to figure out how to get their job done.

In his book, "Turn the Ship Around! A True Story of Turning Followers into Leaders," Captain David Marquet outlines how he implemented the leader to leader model while in charge of the nuclear submarine, the USS Santa Fe. Captain Marquet outlines four primary pillars of the leader to emerging leader model that I believe can be helpful in our examination of the subject of transforming followers into leaders. They are:

> **Control** - Give control, don't take control. This is probably the hardest for most leaders since the more stressful times become, the more we try to control the situation.

> **Competence** - Give your team the tools they need to be technically competent. A technically competent team provides the foundation for trust.

> **Clarity** - State the organization's goals clearly, openly, and honestly. Make sure everyone is working towards the same goals.

> **Courage** - Resist the urge to fall back into the leader to follower model. It is important to continue to trust your team to deliver, even in the face of adversity.

The leader to emerging leader model engages team members in a way that is much more difficult or possibly even impossible with the leader to follower model. When a leadership environment is developed where emerging leaders can be more engaged, and achieve a sense of meaning and purpose in their work the results are extraordinary. As a result of the leader to emerging leader model, retention of rates for emerging leaders improves, collaboration increases, and the organization benefits from empowered workers who take the initiative instead of waiting around to be told what to do.

The leader to leader structure is fundamentally different from the leader to follower structure. At its core is the belief that we can all be leaders, and in fact it's best when we all are leaders. Leadership is not some mystical quality that some possess and others do not. As humans, we all have what it takes, and we all need to use our leadership abilities in every aspect of our work and lives.

An existing leader committed to producing the most impactful type of leadership communicates to people their worth and potential so clearly that they are inspired to see it in themselves. People who are treated as followers have the expectations of followers and act like followers. As followers, they have limited decision-making authority and little incentive to give the best of their intellect, energy, or passion.

Effective leaders know how, when, and most importantly why to empower followers. By empowering the followers in your organization to take responsibility for actions within the scope of their duties, you are allowing those followers to take ownership in those duties, and as a result, morale and performance will naturally increase. Not only will the organization improve under the leader to emerging leader model, but the individuals working within it also became more skilled, knowledgeable, and efficient critical thinkers capable of making excellent and correct decisions with minimal supervisory input.

The process of transforming followers into leaders actually comes down to a leader becoming a people developer. I believe that the opportunity to assist people in their growth and development is the best practice of any leader. A principled leader is a person who works for the benefit of others. Unfortunately, in this day and age that is sometimes not the case. Some leaders are leaders for the purposes of gaining, prestige, fame or wealth. It is not that any of these areas are inherently wrong; however, if the pursuit of these things is at the expense of others or to the neglect of the development of others that can be ultimately detrimental to any organization.

One of the best ways to assist a follower in becoming a leader is to assist them in their self-development. The development of a person's self-image, self-worth, and self-esteem are critical in this process. If a person who has been a follower never sees themselves as something other than a follower, then the motivation to develop into a leader will not be there. We must note here that I don't believe that becoming a leader has anything to do with a title, or a position. A title or a position may come along with certain responsibilities, but if a person does not possess the proper attitude about themselves then the title or the position will not cause them to become a leader or operate effectively as a leader.

In his book, The Spirit of Leadership, Dr. Myles Munroe states that, "there is nothing as powerful as attitude." Attitude dictates your response to the present and determines the quality of your future. You are your attitude, and your attitude is you. If you cannot control your attitude, it will control you." (1) "What is an attitude? It is a mind-set or mental conditioning that determines our interpretation of and response to our environments." (2)

A leader committed to the transformation of followers into leaders also recognizes that there will be times in an emerging leaders journey where the emerging leaders will face the same uncertainties that the existing leaders have faced. Some of those uncertainties include thinking that it is too late to make certain changes after making mistakes or being held back in their development because of past failures. This is a part of the leadership journey. It ebbs and flows. However, an existing leader can use their experiences to encourage and promote the well-being of an emerging leader.

"The leader who influences others to lead or to become leaders is a leader without limitations." (3) This type of leader also realizes that behavior and potential are not necessarily the same things. They believe in the unseen potential of people. When you are an empowering leader an emerging leader will tend to become what you expect them to become. You can literally change a person's life by your attitude and expectations of them. Leaders that are successful in developing the potential of others tend to be people who make the proper assumptions about others. Your assumptions about others are a driving factor in whether or not you see them as emerging leaders or simply followers.

I have been involved with numerous leaders in my lifetime and one of the things that a leader can have a tendency to do is agree with something when they hear it initially or even when they revisit what they have heard. However, the implementation of what we say we are committed too can be an entirely different matter. When it comes to transforming followers into leaders an existing leader cannot think that because they mentally acquiesce to the idea they don't need to consistently and intentionally work at it. "We can't hope for things that we are not currently working on. You will only become what you are becoming right now." (4)

CHAPTER THIRTEEN: REFLECTIONS

A more effective approach to leading today's thought workers is to adopt a leader to emerging leader model and not a leader to follower model.

The leader to emerging leader model engages team members in a way that is much more difficult or possibly even impossible with the leader to follower model.

An existing leader committed to producing the most impactful type of leadership is consistently communicating to people their worth and potential so clearly that they are inspired to see it in themselves.

The process of transforming followers into leaders actually comes down to a leader becoming a people developer.

One of the best ways to assist a follower in becoming a leader is to assist them in their self-development. The development of a person's self-image, self-worth, and self-esteem are critical in this process.

A Word to Emerging Leaders

"Keep your head up, otherwise your crown falls."

Unknown

I have been involved with being a leader and leadership for more than thirty years. There are so many lessons and accounts that I could retell, but the goal of this chapter is to focus on something specific. I could discuss the pillars of leadership, values for leadership, cultivating beliefs that help you grow, mastering your emotions, changing your thoughts, love in action, the principles of self-realization and many others. Yet I want to talk to emerging leaders as though I were talking to my younger self.

What is the one thing that I want to communicate to us? I want to discuss optimism. There will be many challenges in your leadership journey. However, please remember that your leadership journey is really your journey of self-discovery. Without optimism it will be difficult to maintain any momentum when things are moving in the direction that you don't want them to and to overcome any obstacle or setback that you will inevitably face.

Optimism is a not too often discussed subject however, I believe that it is critical to our ultimate leadership success. For what leader can ever achieve their desired goals if they don't believe that in spite of whatever it is that they are facing or have faced they can? What is optimism? The dictionary definition of optimism is a person who is, "disposed to take a favorable view of events and conditions and to expect the most favorable outcome." Other synonyms include words like, confident, expectant, assured, positive, belief, hopeful, and upbeat. Optimism is a disposition and a disposition can be learned. We can learn to have a predominant or a prevailing tendency when it comes to our outlook on life and leadership. It is something that we must choose. It doesn't come to us by default.

PERSONAL LEADERSHIP LESSON

A few years ago I faced the greatest challenge of my life and my leadership. Through a series of poor decisions that I made, I was incarcerated. After being incarcerated, I had some decisions to make. Was I going to give up being a leader or did I believe that leadership was a calling for my life? I knew that leadership was a calling for my life; therefore, I had to make a decision to learn from the unfortunate experiences and maintain an attitude of optimism. Someone asked me, what it was that brought me through that experience and my answer is God and being optimistic about my future.

One of the best illustrations that I have heard concerning optimism comes from General Colin Powell who says that great leaders know things will get better because they themselves will make them better. The following was drilled into Powell during his military training: "Lieutenant, you may be starving, but you must never show hunger. You may be freezing or near heat exhaustion, but you must never show that you are cold or hot. You may be terrified, but you must never show fear. You are the leader and the troops will reflect your emotions." Powell is not an unabashed optimist. He tempers his optimism with logic. "Maybe it can't be done, but always start out believing it can be done until facts and analysis pile up against it. Don't surround yourself with skeptics but don't shut out skeptics who give you solid counterviews."

"Optimism is not about the absence of doubt. It is not about the neglect of reality. It is about one significant driving attitude behind a series of leadership behaviors and that attitude is a consistent positive approach to situations with the intent of looking for and making positive outcomes happen.

There are specific behaviors that are the driving forces behind an optimistic approach. They are as follows:

1. The willingness to consider an idea or opportunity on its own merits.

2. The attitude that approaches ideas and opportunities by attempting to discern what the positive outcomes are.

3. The willingness to listen to multiple viewpoints on "how" to make those outcomes happen before committing to an action.

4. Treating other's viewpoints with openness and dignity.

5. Coming up with the best plan to achieve success.

6. Assessing risks that could de-rail the approach and planning for them appropriately.

7. Making the choice (or recommendation) to proceed based on data, systematic thinking and cost-benefit assessment.

8. When given the opportunity to proceed, devoting not less than your best effort to success.

In essence, optimism and confidence go hand in hand because the optimistic leader has confidence not only in the outcome, but that a good plan to get there exists."

"Optimistic leaders function differently. It is not just a bubbly personality or sunny disposition that makes the optimistic leader different. They actually look at and approach the world in a different way. The half-full attitude of the optimistic leader is seen in the following ways:

They View Things Differently

Optimistic leaders look for opportunities...

Optimistic leaders look for what can be...

Optimistic leaders integrate realism into their optimism...

They Are Genuine

Optimistic leaders believe in others and in possibilities...

Optimistic leaders have learned to distinguish between convictions and preferences...

Optimistic leaders don't like failure but accept it and use it as a part of the process...

Think Outside the Box

Optimistic leaders search for solutions...

Optimistic leaders view obstacles, barriers and failures as problems that cannot be allowed to continue

Optimistic leaders are open to new thinking...

Positively Impact Others

Optimistic leaders are inspiring in the belief that success is possible...

Optimistic leaders are both magnetic and contagious...

Optimistic leader's attitudes inspire enthusiasm and effort...

Impact The Environment

Optimistic leaders create an atmosphere in which innovation and engagement flourish…

Optimistic leaders build networks between people…

Optimistic leaders break down the isolated mentality…

Want to see Individual and Organizational Growth

Optimism divorced from reality is not believable. The proof of the optimistic leader is ultimately in execution and this is where the optimistic leader's co-workers can potentially encounter problems and difficulties with him or her. The optimistic leader couples their attitude that a solution can be found with the act of rolling up their sleeves to help find it. Ultimately, optimism without movement creates the belief that possibility is just talk and that is the point that the leader begins to lose credibility.

Optimistic leaders can also be their own worst enemies if they do not learn to assess and live within their performance capacities. The optimistic leader does not like to say "no" and as a result, there can be significant demands on their time and energy. These demands create stress that can change the optimistic leader's outlook because the leader cannot give the time and attention to thinking through a situation before they have to commit." In his book, "Learned Optimism," psychologist Martin Seligman informs us that the way that we interpret the events in our lives and understand the effects these interpretations will have, we realize that we can choose to look at our lives, obstacles, or setbacks in a different light. At the core of pessimism is a feeling of helplessness, that nothing we do will make a difference. It is true that there are many things outside of our control. Equally true is that there are also many things within our control. Our attitudes and choices will affect the actions that we take, the way that we interact with others, and how we will proceed in life.

CHAPTER FOURTEEN: REFLECTIONS

The dictionary definition of optimism is a person who is, "disposed to take a favorable view of events and conditions and to expect the most favorable outcome."

Optimism is not about the absence of doubt. It is not about the neglect of reality. It is about one significant driving attitude behind a series of leadership behaviors and that attitude is a consistent positive approach to situations with the intent of looking for and making positive outcomes happen.

Optimistic leaders look at and approach the world in a different way.

The way that we interpret the events in our lives and understand the effects these interpretations will have, we realize that we can choose to look at our lives, obstacles, or setbacks in a different light.

PART THREE

PROJECT LEADERSHIP

Online Market Leadership through Reverse Engineering

S o you want to be a market leader? What exactly does it mean to lead your market anyway?

For some of you it means that your company's products or services are first in the mind of a consumer, for others it means dominating your local or global market in terms of volume of sales of goods and services or perhaps you desire to be the largest producer of value in your particular market.

Your objective might also be project related. For example, if you are the head of product innovation or strategy within a major corporation, it might be necessary for you to devise a game plan for market domination.

Regardless of what your desire to lead in your market, I would like to suggest that you consider taking a <u>reverse engineered</u> approach.

Reverse Engineering

In laymen's terms, reverse engineering means that you take a look at your competitor's products, services or strategies and legally replicate the systems which have proven to be successful.

Here's is what businessdictionary.com has to say about the meaning of reverse engineering, it's worth noting:

Legally sanctioned <u>method</u> of <u>copying</u> a <u>technology</u> which (as opposed to starting from scratch) begins with an existing product and <u>works</u> backward to figure out how it does what it does. When the <u>product's</u> basic <u>principle</u> or core <u>concept</u> is determined, the next step is to reproduce the same results by employing different mechanisms to avoid any (legally forbidden) patent infringement. A common practice worldwide, reverse engineering is responsible for the ubiquitous 'IBM Compatible' computers, and is called emulation in software industry.

Read more: http://www.businessdictionary.com/definition/reverse-engineering.html#ixzz4DZfNziWO

Now some people believe that it's better to be first when it comes to creating products or services within their market. But I strongly urge you to reconsider the understanding that it might be more profitable to come behind your competitors who have already paved the way and then make subtle changes to capture market share.

After all, someone once said that "Pioneers die with arrows in their backs". That's because those who enter a market first are usually the ones to engage in costly trial and error, only to realize that their competitors come behind them and destroy them after they realize what the "pioneer" (the person who was first) did successfully.

Sun Tzu put it best when he said, "it's better to attack your enemies plans than it is to destroy his army". When reverse engineering your competitor's successful strategies, you are ultimately leveraging the time, money and resources that another company has used for your own competitive advantage.

Through this process, you can quickly discover what your competitors have done profitably and plug the holes in their strategy and come up with something better.

In this chapter, I will go into both academic and real world detail about how this works. So let me give you a quick example of how this can be powerfully used straight away.

All major companies like Amazon, Starbucks and McDonalds have something called conversion funnels. A conversion funnel is basically an automated sequence of systems setup to strategically attract More customers into your business that are more valuable and yet less expensive to acquire.

At our company, Ignited Results, we routinely build conversion funnels for our clients by first starting with reverse engineering our client's competitor's funnels and then we build a custom funnel for our client based upon a model that has already proven itself to be profitable and I recommend you consider doing the same.

A simplified version of a conversion funnel would begin with a targeted ad placed somewhere online where your customers are already hanging out. This could be a chat room, forum, blog or targeted social media.

In a few paragraphs I will show you exactly where to place your ads to guarantee that your specific targeted customers will see it.

The targeted ad would draw the user to your sales page which will offer the visitor a "freebie" or low cost offer designed to get the visitor to give up their name and email address or purchase something from you at a low introductory rate.

After the visitor has made a purchase they are your customer for life if nurtured properly through a return path, such as follow up emails or re-targeted ads that follow them around cyber space.

These conversion funnel systems are literally responsible for producing billions of dollars in annual revenue for major companies and they are quietly making fortunes for regular everyday entrepreneurs around the globe when properly setup.

It can cost you a small fortune to do all the testing to determine exactly where to advertise. Further, it can also cost as much as $30,000 for ad design and then you would spend several thousands of dollars more on testing which ads bring in the highest number of customers at the lowest dollar upfront investment.

If you were first in your market - the pioneer - you would have to spend even more time and money testing your sales pages to see which sequences, make the most money when a visitor lands on your site.

But I can show you how to ethically appropriate $1,000,000 worth of competitor research for under $100 bucks by following the steps outlined within the next few paragraphs.

By taking a reverse engineered approach you can use tools like similarweb.com. Simply input your competitor's website and it will tell you which ads they use and more importantly where they advertise, which ads convert the highest number of visitors to customers and give you a look at their online conversion funnel systems, sales pages and more so you can replicate their success.

You must do this ethically because I'm not suggesting for you to duplicate content but more so replicate strategy that has already proven to be profitable. At IgnitedResults.com we often take this approach when building conversion funnels for our clients because it saves them thousands and in some cases millions of dollars in ad design, copyrighting, testing etc.

Reverse engineering is powerful not only because it tells you what your competitors are doing and lets you know in advance what strategies work profitably, but also because it takes you into the mind of your customer specifically and reveals to you the thoughts, insights and desires of your customers and that my friend is **awesomely powerful!**

John Romero put it best when he said *"You're headed in the right direction when you realize the customer viewpoint is more important than the company viewpoint. It's more productive to learn from your customers instead of about them."*

So far I have given you a summary of how reverse engineering works and in the following pages of this chapter I will explain some of the technical steps involved as well as some more in-depth specific strategies that you may use on your own or at least know what to look for when hiring a professional digital marketing firm.

It is important to ensure that no copyrighted structures of objects are duplicated to avoid facing the arms of law especially from a competitor whom may decide to take a legal action against you and your business. However, there are occasions where some of the copyright laws may not apply and therefore they are not subject to legal battles especially in systems that are used to market and optimize websites.

Reverse Engineering is typically composed of certain basic steps, although they can vary when looking at the specifics at each step. They include

- Observing and assessing the mechanisms used and how systems operate.

- Dissecting and studying the inner functions of a mechanical or a technical device.

- Comparing the original device with the observations that have been made and later suggest possible improvements on it.

By using reverse technology, it is possible for a researcher to assemble any necessary technical data for the purpose of documenting the technological operations or the components of the system. Furthermore, when researchers are doing reverse engineering on software, they are able to study and understand the strength of a particular system and identify any possible weaknesses in terms of security and interoperability. Through this process, the researchers are able to understand the working of a program and the major aspects of the program that may cause it not to work. Through reverse technology, independent manufacturers can do well in competitive markets by improving the dominant products. An example where reverse engineering is used is where security audits are performed on software to increase the quality of protection on the systems and related networks by revealing any flaws. Often, interoperability of existing designs and creation of better designs begins with reverse engineering. However, for this case reverse engineering of marketing systems of competitors is one of the crucial applications of reverse engineering. There are different ways by which reverse engineering your competitors marketing systems can be done and the following are some of the ways to use to be on top of the process.

The Site Structure

The first and most important element is the site structure. Having information architecture of a website and general structure of the site is a key factor in good performance of an organic search. It is usually divided into various aspects:

- Page depth

- Internal structure of the links

- Following the best practice from a technical viewpoint

- Availing better user experience to intensify the chances of retaining customers.

After scrutinizing your site structure, the next step is to now look at your competitor's multiple elements through comparative analysis and therefore come up with more conclusive statements to help you be on top. Here are some of the elements which have been looked at:

Identify Your Actual Competitors

This is the first step in reverse engineering. Most people might think that identification of competitors is obvious but it is tougher than you may think. It is important to have a clear idea of who your direct competitors are i.e. those that provide a product or service that is almost identical to yours. It is important to ask yourself how aware you are on your perceived and indirect competitors.

For example, there exists indirect competition between service providers such as web designers and other 'do it yourself services' such as WordPress, which can be downloaded. All these services aim at satisfying the need for a website by a customer. Analysing the keywords will assist in revealing your indirect competitors. This plays an important role in helping you determine competitors that have product terms that are similar to your terms.

Perceived competitors are the most difficult to identify. These competitors are not in the same industry as you and they don't offer products or services that are similar to yours but they compete for the same customer's time and energy that is used while enjoying your products. For example, in the past, mobile phones had a different market from that of digital cameras but in recent years, Kodak started competing with phone manufacturers the minute the first camera phone was introduced.

After assembling and organizing a list of all types of competitors, you should narrow it down to 3-5 and begin your analysis. Note that you should cover all types of competitors.

Information Architecture

It is essential for you to study and understand how your competitors have structured their websites when compared to yours. This will increase your knowledge and understanding of how their websites have been set up which is important for customer's journeys, in addition to improving organic search. In order to get a detailed understanding of the structuring of your competitor's websites, it is important to perform a ScreamingFrog crawl on their websites and aid the "tree" view. The view gives you the design of the Information Architecture (IA) and indicates how the links are passed from the main domain to other parts of the website.

It is important that you consider the following key factors when comparing your IA competitors:

i.   The depth of the URLs/pages that rank the major keywords compared to yours.

ii.   The size of the IA, is it much smaller? If it is smaller how much wide spread?

iii.   How the structure of the URL functions with the infrastructure architecture e.g. are they URLs kept closer to the Domain than that of your website?

There are several important questions that you should ask yourself. For instance, which phrases or keywords are being used by your competitors? What topics are they majoring on most? In their calls for action, what type of language do they mostly use? Examining the methods used by the competitor to attract traffic and build quality backlinks will save you a lot of trial and error and help you create a masterpiece that will give the best results.

Analyzing the Competitors Technical SEO Strategy

Doing an analysis of the technical SEO of your competitors can enable you to locate any techniques that you have not utilized. It is important to start with the basics. These include:

- Are their titles being tagged correctly?

- Do they make use of the content from multimedia to keep readers on their sites?

- Do they use keywords without stuffing?

After scrutinizing the site for these factors, you can now dig deeper into advanced forms of SEO. It is possible that your competitors have been using onsite techniques that your site is lacking and hence making it hard for you to outdo them e.g. websites on HTTPs can apply the HSTs which assures the search engines of site security. Use of accelerated mobile changes or AMP will help to improve the speed of the loads on mobile devices. JSON Schema is one of the most advanced ways that you can use to mark up your website with java and hence make it flexible. It might be difficult for you to catch up with your competitors if your code is not as advanced as their code or if your site is slower. It is imperative for you to get clued in on SEO techniques that are much advanced or make use of technical SEO pro to make a review of your competitors and at the same time locate possible opportunities that you can employ in your strategy.

User Experience (UX): Page level analysis

In analyzing technical SEO strategy, it's also important to look at the page level UX of your competitor's highly ranking website. This is as far as all the components of UX are involved including readability (Flesch Kincaid Grade Level, Dale-Chall, Smog Index and Gunning Fog). These are very important as they expose how your content compares to your competitors in terms of ease of reading.

More importantly, is your page speed both mobile and desktop? One thing that you need to know is that, since Google launched the mobile algorithm update, priority has essentially moved to the page speed especially at mobile side. Most of the high ranking websites utilize the mobile user experience considering that most of the customers use mobile mostly for navigation and if the page speed is magnificent so is the mobile user experience. The user experience can be provided by the URL Profiler, which uses different metrics and analyses the technical elements i.e. Content length, Text to HTML Ratio, HTML length etc.; on-page content i.e. paragraph count, word count, reading time etc.; content score i.e. Dale-Chall Score, Flesch Kincaid Reading Ease etc. and finally the mobile friendliness aspect. All these mentioned metrics that can be compiled using the URL profiler which essentially determines how your competitor's website is heavily coded based on the mentioned metrics.

Analyze The Competitors Link Building Strategy

In reverse engineering backlinks, it is vital to do a thorough analysis and evaluation of the subject matter. The process analyzes the competitive backlinks and involves examining who links to the website of your competitor and the design of their pages. This makes it possible for anyone to learn and understand why backlinks are so valuable. This could be as a result of the anchor text, domain page rank, the link list or the quality content that surrounds the link.

It is also very essential for you to study the destination of the links and the content that is shown on the pages of your competitors. However, it is important that you keep it in mind that it is illegal to directly copy the content. You should just use the content for the purpose of research. After establishing the points, you should evaluate the pairing quality and decide whether adding such a link to your site adds value to it. Make sure that you only select the best backlinks for your site as they will greatly boost the SEO of your website. Remember that spam and poor quality links will basically be picked by the algorithms of Google which may poorly rank your site.

It is possible to see which sites are being used by your competitors to create their backlinks by using various tools such as SEOpen. This tool shows you the links as indexed by Google, Yahoo and MSN. It also makes it possible for you to visit those specific links and view the type of content being used by your competitors e.g. when the SEOpen tool shows the links being built by your competitors from a site that submits articles, it is possible for you to click on those links and have a look of the articles being created and published by the competitors. This will also help in finding appropriate websites which you can link to. Make sure that you study and understand the sites which are mostly used by your competitors because there are great chances that they are getting quality traffic from such sites.

When it comes to seeing an overview of the structure of your internal link, there are many ways which you can use. The best method that you can use is the internal links reports of the Google Webmaster tools, which you can easily download. However, it is not possible to access the webmaster tools account of your competitors. In case you want to access the links, you can do it by running a ScreamingFrog crawl on their sites and do a bulk export of all the in links. By this, all manual links from the website will be exported. By use of basic filters, you can replicate any links produced by the webmaster tools for your own site. This is very important especially when analyzing the inbound links.

Reverse Engineering the Sales Funnel

Reverse engineering the sales funnel is based on understanding the different prospects that are required for you to be able to attain your revenue goals. Therefore, by reverse engineering your competitor's sale funnel you will be able to determine if a selected market is large enough for you. Some of the most significant elements that you should accomplish before embarking on the reverse engineering of sales funnel include looking at significant data in regard to economic reports, census data and competitor's information among others.

There are significant steps which you could apply in reverse engineering sales funnels. This includes drawing a funnel and dividing the funnel into the following categories as demonstrated below:

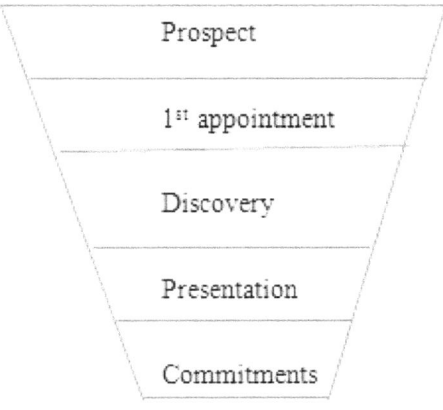

The next step here is to figure out how to close the ratios that are in each step. For instance, using an example to illustrate below:

The prospects to 1st appointments could be 10% while the first appointments to discoveries can be 50%. The discoveries to presentations assuming is 50% and finally the presentations to commitments may be 50% as well. With these numbers you can now reverse engineer them. First you will need to put the number of those customers or clients that you will wish to have by the end of the year in the funnels commitment portion, and then you will go backwards in order to obtain the total number of prospects.

Most successful Internet based marketers mostly apply sales funnels to ensure their businesses are on track. The strategy that is used varies among different businesses and that's why one should do a comparative analysis before going to reverse engineer the sales funnel. The sales funnels are quite important in marketing one's business. For instance, most of them use different of the competitors use different strategies to redirect their users to their sales pages i.e. through opt-in pages that require email submission for building of email lists. The sales pages are the place where all the marketing action occurs. These pages can be either video sales pages or written sales pages. One thing that you need to note of your competitor's page is the eye catching graphics and pictures as well as products descriptions. Therefore, you need to optimize the sale pages to make sure that it doesn't draw negative attention but rather positively attract customers to your page. This can be borrowed greatly from looking at the competitor's sales pages and how they are able to do their sale funnels and then apply a similar basic principle to their actions.

Mobile and the Organic Search Visibility

One of the best methods that can be used to gauge the organic performance of your competitors is to study and analyze the visibility of their search. Various tools can be used for this analysis: SearchMetrics,

SISTRIX, SEMrush etc. the visibility for searches is measured by the phrases or keywords that a site ranks for, the click through rate that is assigned to their rank position and the volume of the keywords used.

Recently, mobile visibility was introduced by SearchMetrics which is very significant as it highlights any possible discrepancies between mobile and desktop organic visibility e.g. if the organic visibility of desktops was higher than mobile, this shows that the site is not mobile friendly. The SearchMetrics can also be used as a comparison tool which reveals how organic visibility of websites compares to others.

Analyze what could be missing

This strategy has proven to be the most valuable strategy that can be used to analyze any competition. Basically, it looks for any needs within the target market that are not being fulfilled by your competitors. These needs include. availability of forums where your competitors' services and products are being discussed by their customers and availability of reviews about the services and products of your competitors and any missing service that you can provide that is not provided currently by the competitors. This will greatly help you to identify any untapped opportunity and therefore the easy and most convenient way to gain an upper hand.

The most important thing you should know

Any competition that takes place on the Internet leaves traces. The source of traffic and the optimization that is made by the competing companies is mainly public. Any tactic that is used by your competitors to increase their visibility is also visible to you. It is important to examine the activities of your competitors and then reverse engineer their strategies in a more thoughtful and tactical way. By doing that, you are able to enhance your efforts and mimic their successes.

The process of comparing the performance of your SEO with that of competitors is am established practice. There are many manuals and tools that can help you do the analysis and comparison. They analyze the quantity and quality of the backlinks. The tools use services such as: Scorecard, Open Site Explorer, Alexa, Quantcast, SEOmoz, Google Trends and Whois.net. You can use these tools to compare the competitors' sites with your website. By using the tools, you are able to see which company scores the best and on which metrics and how their revenue is impacted.

In addition, it is important that you understand the online marketing strategies of the competitors as it helps to reverse engineer their strategies. This task can be time consuming but Audenti has simplified it by giving a simpler option. Traditionally, different analysis tools would be used but with Audenti, 'competitors' analytics' can be used. The analytics is composed of all the tools that watch the performance of other sites. All you need is just to click.

You can follow the promotional activities of the competitors. By this, it is possible to react to changes and anticipate any potential move. Examine and study the keywords and phrases that the competitors are ranking for, look for any keywords that they are using in their adverts and learn the source of their backlinks.

Growth Through Strategy

"Strategy is a style of thinking, a conscious and deliberate process, an intensive implementation system, the science of insuring future success."

Pete Johnson

How can we learn to plan more effectively and avoid unpleasant surprises? The answer is strategy. Strategy or strategic thinking is an essential tool in leadership because it is a way of peering into the future with confidence that our actions today will yield the best possible outcome tomorrow. It is the commitment to building towards a long-term perspective. Any beneficial activity or organization that is lasting requires careful planning. Strategy also requires the skills for problem-solving, and critical decision-making.

Strategy can be utilized in every aspect of life. It doesn't matter if it is the development of your long-term family plan or if it is the strategic plan for the corporation of which you are the C.E.O.. The principles that are utilized for growth through strategy are generally universal. For example, the quarterback of a football team has to learn how to utilize the talents of the players on their team, make adjustments based upon what the other team's defense is doing against his team, identify opportunities on a given play, and most of all, he has to know what the basic play is before the team breaks from the huddle. He has to have an idea of what play they want to run to lead them down the field for a touchdown. That play may have to be adjusted; however, they at least as an offensive team have a common starting place with the common goal of scoring a touchdown.

Strategy is a cultivated skill. No one is born with a fully developed ability to think in a strategic manner. It is a skill that must be cultivated and practiced. Unfortunately, many people are stuck in the mode of cognitive confinement or static thinking; they consciously reject thinking about tomorrow. The antithesis of strategic thinking is to continue doing what you have always done, the same way that you have always done it and then expect to get different results. Albert Einstein called this type of thinking a form of insanity. Strategic thinking or strategy demands that you engage a methodical process of questioning, evaluating, making assumptions, gathering information, analyzing and planning so that you can take action.

At some point we all think about the future, but there can be a significant difference in how we think about it. If I think about the future in terms of what it may be, then I am simply daydreaming. If I think about the future in the context of goals and a long-range plan to reach those goals and plans based upon careful analysis, then I am thinking strategically.

The term strategy refers to more than just a plan. "Strategy is a method or plan that we craft to bring about a desired future. It is a plan that assesses, acquires and allocates necessary resources to the most effective and efficient use. It is a way of perceiving and considering the future with our aims and goals in mind. It is also a way of dealing with a constantly changing environment, both responding to that environment to achieve our goals and attempting, where possible, to change that environment to the benefit of ourselves and others." **(1)**

PROJECT LEADERSHIP LESSON

I have learned that when it comes to strategy, the best strategy is developed with many different perspectives. A comprehensive strategy cannot be developed with only one leader's ideas.

Thinking strategically assists us in making sense out of chaotic situations and enables us to use the forces around us to our advantage, rather than allow those forces to use us. In essence, strategy equips us with tools that help us meet the future with confidence. A common analytical tool used in strategic planning is called a SWOT analysis (strengths, weaknesses, opportunities and threats). It is an analytical tool that helps us to look at all aspects of a situation to ensure that our strategic intent matches our resources and capabilities. Strategic thinking means acting from knowledge, not emotion or preconceptions.

"A challenge that crops up repeatedly, in your work or personal life, is likely a systemic problem. Strategic thinking enables us to recognize the symptoms of what Peter Drucker called the "recurring crisis," to unwind the problem, and to tackle the underlying systemic issue. In this way, we can often construct our own conscious systems to solve the pathology of systemic problems. When it comes to project leadership, it is important to recognize that systems are interconnected and dependent on one another to function. Consider the systems that support us: garbage collection, food distribution, public transportation, fuel for automobiles, electrical grids, police departments, manufacturing assembly lines, the legal system, cell phones, the Internet, water systems and so on. Everything in our world happens in the context of a system. One action in one part of a system influences throughout the system." (**2**)

A good test for determining whether you have identified a truly systemic problem that may hinder your projects from fully developing is to ask the question "Why?" at least five times. Such a series of questions forces us to keep going until we reach the truly systemic cause. Once you have identified the problem, the next task is to look for creative ways to solve it or avoid it.

Projects are not just operational they are also interconnected to the people who are a part of them. If the systems that are in place are not effective in assisting the people who are a part of the project, then the project will not reach its highest potential. So the million-dollar question is, "why do some projects succeed and others fail? That really is the million-dollar question, isn't it? I think about it all the time. Thankfully, there are concrete answers.

According to Steven Key, if you are frustrated that one of your projects just can't seem to get off the ground, it might be because these practices aren't being followed:

1. Set a timeline.

Every project you start must have an end date. Be realistic about how much time a project will take to accomplish. If you budget too little time, you may end up feeling defeated. If you consistently budget too much of your time for projects, you will get a lot less done than you're capable of.

If you are unsure what steps should be taken to achieve your goal and so can't create a realistic timeline, start by asking questions. Only when you have a firm grasp about what needs to be done, can you start setting effective project deadlines.

2. Get everyone on the same page.

You can't do some projects on your own. So assemble a team before starting the project and let every member of the group know what you will need from them. If people don't understand what's expected of them, they won't be able to deliver.

Go a step further and be sure that members of the team understand the big picture. What's the goal of the project? How will you achieve it? Why is each person's contribution important?

Even before sitting down with the team for a meeting, send an agenda in advance. Never end a meeting with the team without cementing the steps that must be taken next and who's responsible for them.

3. Hold regular meetings.

Setting a timeline and clarifying who is responsible for what isn't enough. You must keep people accountable by regularly checking in with them. You can use project tools to track progress and to keep abreast of what everyone is up to. It functions like a scorecard: Everyone is aware of what's getting done and who's doing it.

It is obvious when someone is falling behind. This makes it easy for someone else to step in and volunteer to help out. At your meetings, review the project tracker and talk about what is working and what isn't. Keep your meetings short and don't veer from the agenda.

4. Key players should make themselves available.

If you want to make sure a project gets done, force everyone who is taking part to be accessible. Do your part by leading by example. Respond to emails and phone calls promptly. When you have so much going on, it's easy for something to slip through the cracks. The easiest way to avoid that is to be accessible and respond promptly.

5. Promote transparency.

Whether the news is good or bad, members of your team will work harder when they feel they are in the know. Do all that you can to encourage the people you work with to take ownership of the project.

"Another thing to examine is that strategic planning in projects is both an art and a science. When a project stalls, here are four questions you should ask yourself. The answers will help you think more productively and make significant progress faster.

<u>The Art</u>

What do you want to be known for?

This is your time to be vulnerable. Research professor Brené Brown says it best. "Vulnerability is the birthplace of innovation, creativity and change."

When we allow ourselves to be vulnerable and open to what it is we truly want, then we are able to make forward movement. Be willing to think in terms of what is needed first as you craft this idea onto paper. This is your time to not only self-identify with the project you want to start, but soul-identify. Be your most vulnerable self as you answer the ultimate question of "why."

Who do you know who is known for that?

Think of someone who is already doing something similar to the project you want to start, and reach out to them. This may seem forward and presumptuous, but consider the potential positive outcomes it will have. Introduce yourself and let them know what you're working on, or hoping to begin working on. Engage in fluid conversation that allows you to learn from them. Odds are, they will be more than happy to hear from you, help guide you and cheer for you along the way.

Oprah Winfrey's definition of a mentor is absolutely right -- "a mentor is someone who allows you to see the hope inside yourself." Reaching out to this person will not only get your wheels spinning, but it will feed your soul as you begin to recognize your potential and ability to get this project started.

The Science

What are the next three milestones?

Identify three significant aspects of the overall goal you hope to achieve. These will be your subprojects. Add these subprojects to your to-do list about 30 days apart. Each week, review the subproject and choose something you can do next to achieve that part of the overall goal. Often, making a phone call, reviewing a white paper or drafting a letter is just what it takes to create a little momentum that goes a long way. Celebrate these victories along the way. They will keep your fire lit.

What can you automate, delegate or eliminate?

Find time to study your own ways of getting things done. Are there things you can automate, delegate or eliminate? "If you want to do a few small things right, do them yourself. If you want to do great things and make a big impact, learn to delegate." Let this quote by author John C. Maxwell inspire you to do great things.

Maybe it is a task that you can outsource. By outsourcing this task, you will not only be creating more time in your schedule to begin tackling the project, but you will be providing a new opportunity for someone else to do something great." (**3**)

Make getting started easier by considering the art and science behind it all. Be vulnerable, celebrate the victories and make room for what is to come. Go get the momentum that you need for your project!

CHAPTER FIFTEEN: REFLECTIONS

Strategy or strategic thinking is an essential tool in leadership because it is a way of peering into the future with confidence that our actions today will yield the best possible outcome tomorrow.

Strategy can be utilized in every aspect of life. It doesn't matter if it is the development of your long-term family plan or if it is the strategic plan for the corporation that you are the C.E.O. of.

Strategy is a cultivated skill. No one is born with a fully developed ability to think in a strategic manner.

The antithesis of strategic thinking is to continue doing what you have always done, the same way that you have always done it and then expect to get different results.

A good test for determining whether you have identified a truly systemic problem that may hinder your projects from fully developing is to ask the question "Why?" at least five times.

Projects are not just operational; they are also interconnected to the people who are a part of them.

CHAPTER SIXTEEN

Producing Organizational Change Through Projects

"The secret of change is to focus all of your energy, not on fighting the old, but on building the new."

Socrates

"Successful organizations develop a culture that keeps adjusting consistently. This can present some senior leaders with an unfamiliar challenge. When there is the potential for a major transformation in an enterprise, a number of senior leaders feel most comfortable devising the strategic and tactical plans. However, to fully succeed they must also have an intimate understanding of the human side of change. The alignment of the organizations culture, values, people and behaviors – to encourage the desired results. Plans exclusively do not capture value; value is realized only through sustained, collective actions of the people who are responsible for designing, executing and living out a changed environment.

There is no single methodology that fits every organization, but there are a set of practices, tools and techniques that can be adapted to a variety of situations. These are practices that are a systematic, comprehensive framework, that leaders can understand what to expect and how to manage their own personal change and how to engage the entire organization in the process.

First, **the human aspect needs to be addressed systematically**. Any significant transformation creates "people issues." For a project to be successful people will have to step up, responsibilities may be changed, new skills and capabilities must be developed and there will be some uncertainties or even resistance. Dealing with these issues on a reactive basis causes speed, morale and results to be at risk. A formal approach for managing change that begins with the leadership team engages the key stakeholders in the organization and then can be adapted throughout the organization. Change in this instance must be based upon a realistic assessment of the organization's history, readiness and capacity to change.

Second, **change starts at the top.** Since change is inherently unsettling for people at all levels of an organization when it is on the horizon, all eyes will turn to the leader(s) and the leadership team for strength, support, and direction. The leaders themselves must embrace the new approaches first, both to challenge and to motivate the rest of the organization. They must speak with one voice and model the desired behaviors. The executive team also needs to understand that, although its public face may be one of unity, it, too, is composed of individuals who are going through various experiences and need to be supported.

Executive teams that work well together are best positioned for success. They are aligned and committed to the direction of change, understand the culture and behaviors the changes intend to introduce, and can model those changes themselves. Only after the leadership team goes through the process of aligning and committing to the change initiative will the work force be able to deliver desired results.

Third, **involve every layer of the organization.** As transformation programs progress from defining strategy and setting targets to design and implementation, they affect different levels of the organization. Change efforts must include plans for identifying leaders throughout the organization and pushing responsibility for design and implementation down, so that change permeates through the organization. At each layer of the organization, the leaders who are identified and trained must be aligned to the organization's vision, equipped to execute their specific mission, and motivated to make change happen.

Fourth, **make the formal case to the emerging leaders.** Individuals are inherently rational and will question to what extent change is needed, whether the organization is headed in the right direction, and whether they want to commit personally to making change happen. They will look to the leadership for answers. The articulation of a formal case for change and the creation of a written vision statement are invaluable opportunities to create or compel leadership-team alignment.

Three steps should be followed in developing the case: First, confront reality and articulate a convincing need for change. Second, demonstrate faith that the organization has a viable future and the leadership to get there. Finally, provide a road map to guide behavior and decision making. Leaders must then customize this message for various internal audiences, describing the pending change in terms that matter to the individuals.

PROJECT LEADERSHIP LESSON

I have always enjoyed the development aspect of projects. What I have learned is that most projects are tied to people and therefore, need to be continually evaluated to make sure that the welfare of people is at the forefront of the project. It can be easy to forget the primary reason for projects if we don't remind ourselves.

Fifth, **create ownership.** Leaders of large change programs must over-perform during the transformation and be the zealots who create a critical mass among the work force in favor of change. This requires more than mere buy-in or passive agreement that the direction of change is acceptable. It demands ownership by leaders willing to accept responsibility for making change happen in all of the areas they influence or control. Ownership is often best created by involving people in identifying problems and crafting solutions. It is reinforced by incentives and rewards. These can be tangible or psychological.

Sixth, **communicate the message.** Too often, change leaders make the mistake of believing that others understand the issues, feel the need to change, and see the new direction as clearly as they do. The best change programs reinforce core messages through regular, timely advice that is both inspirational and practical. Communication flows in from the bottom and out from the top, and must be targeted to provide people in the organization with the right information at the right time and to solicit their input and feedback. Often this will require over communication through multiple channels.

Seventh, **assess the cultural environment of the organization.** Successful change programs pick up speed and intensity as they cascade down, making it critically important that leaders understand and account for culture and behaviors at each level of the organization. Companies often make the mistake of assessing culture either too late or not at all. Thorough cultural diagnostics can assess organizational readiness to change, bring major problems to the surface, identify conflicts, and define factors that can recognize and influence sources of leadership and resistance. These diagnostics identify the core values, beliefs, behaviors, and perceptions that must be taken into account for successful change to occur. They serve as the common baseline for designing essential change elements, such as the new corporate vision, and building the infrastructure and programs needed to drive change.

Eighth, **address culture intentionally.** Once the culture is understood, it should be addressed as thoroughly as any other area in a change program. Leaders should be explicit about the culture and underlying behaviors that will best support the new way of doing business, and find opportunities to model and reward those behaviors. This requires developing a baseline, defining an explicit end-state or desired culture, and devising detailed plans to make the transition.

Organizational culture is an amalgam of shared history, explicit values and beliefs, and common attitudes and behaviors. Change programs can involve creating a culture, combining cultures, or reinforcing cultures. Understanding that all organizations have a cultural center — the focus of thought, activity, influence, or personal identification — is often an effective way to jump-start cultural change.

Ninth, **prepare for the unexpected.** No change program goes completely according to plan. People react in unexpected ways; areas of anticipated resistance fall away; and the external environment shifts. Effectively managing change requires continual reassessment of its impact and the organization's willingness and ability to adopt the next wave of transformation. Fed by real data from the field and supported by information and solid decision-making processes, change leaders can then make the adjustments necessary to maintain momentum and drive results.

Tenth, **speak to the individual.** Change is both an institutional journey and a very personal one. Some people spend many hours working in an organization; many think of their colleagues as a second family. Individuals (or teams of individuals) need to know how their work will change, what is expected of them during and after the change program, how they will be measured, and what success or failure will mean for them and those around them. Team leaders should be as honest and explicit as possible. People will react to what they see and hear around them, and need to be involved in the change process. Highly visible rewards, such as promotion, recognition, and bonuses, should be provided as dramatic reinforcement for embracing change. Sanction or removal of people standing in the way of change will reinforce the institution's commitment.

Most leaders contemplating change know that people matter. It is all too tempting, however, to dwell on the plans and processes, which don't talk back and don't respond emotionally, rather than face up to the more difficult and more critical human issues. But mastering the "soft" side of change management does not need to be a mystery." (**1**)

CHAPTER SIXTEEN: REFLECTIONS

Successful organizations develop a culture that keeps adjusting consistently.

There is no single methodology that fits every organization, but there are a set of practices, tools and techniques that can be adapted to a variety of situations.

Notes

Chapter One:

1. Joe Dimaggio, M.D.: Conversations that Matter/Insights and Distinctions. San Francisco, CA: Landmark Essays, Volume 1, 2001

2. Ibid.

3. Ibid.

4. Hitendra Wadhwa: Personal Leadership Program/Science of Self. New York, NY: Institute for Personal Leadership, 2014

5. Ibid.

6. Ibid.

7. Stephen R. Covey: Principled Centered Leadership. New York, NY: Free Press, 1990

8. Bill George: Authentic Leadership. Hoboken, NJ, Jossey-Bass, 2004

Chapter Two:

1. Hitendra Wadhwa: Personal Leadership Program/Science of Self. New York, NY: Institute for Personal Leadership, 2014

2. Dr. Myles Munroe: The Spirit of Leadership. New Kensington, PA: Whitaker House Publishers, 2005

3. Hitendra Wadhwa: Personal Leadership Program/Science of Self. New York, NY: Institute for Personal Leadership, 2014

4. Ibid.

5. Tom Marshall: Understanding Leadership. Grand Rapids, MI: Baker Book House Company, 1991

6. Hitendra Wadhwa: Personal Leadership Program/Science of Self. New York, NY: Institute for Personal Leadership, 2014

Chapter Three:

1. Dr. Myles Munroe: The Spirit of Leadership. New Kensington, PA: Whitaker House Publishers, 2005

Chapter Four:

1. Stephen R. Covey: Principled Centered Leadership. New York, NY: Free Press, 1990
2. Steve Zaffron and Dave Logan. The Three Laws of Performance. San Francisco, CA: Jossey-Bass, 2009

Chapter Five:

1. C.W. Von Bergen, Barlow Soper and Buddy Gaster. Effective Self-Management, Volume 14, Number 2. Journal of Business and Entrepreneurship, 2002
2. Dr. Myles Munroe: The Spirit of Leadership. New Kensington, PA: Whitaker House Publishers, 2005
3. Stephen R. Covey: Principled Centered Leadership. New York, NY: Free Press, 1990
4. Bruce McArthur: Your Life: Why It Is The Way It Is and What You Can Do About It. Virginia Beach, VA: A.R.E. Press, 1993

Chapter Six:

1. Ralph Jacobson: Getting Unstuck: Using Leadership Paradox To Execute Confidence. New York, NY: Productivity Press, 2013
2. Ibid.

Chapter Seven:

1. Strong's Concordance: Nashville, TN: Thomas Nelson Publishing, 2010
2. Grigori Raiport: Red Gold. New York, NY: Tarcher Publishing, 1988

3. Ibid.

4. Ibid.

5. Ibid.

6. Dr. Myles Munroe: The Spirit of Leadership. New Kensington, PA: Whitaker House Publishers, 2005

7. Ibid.

Chapter Eight:

1. Dr. Myles Munroe: The Spirit of Leadership. New Kensington, PA: Whitaker House Publishers, 2005

2. Deepak Chopra: The Soul of Leadership. New York, NY: Harmony Books, 2010

Chapter Nine:

1. James M. Kouzes and Barry Z. Posner: The Leadership Challenge. San Francisco, CA: Jossey-Bass, 2008

2. Ibid.

3. Ibid.

4. Ibid.

5. Ibid.

Chapter Ten:

1. Steve Zaffron and Dave Logan: The Three Laws of Performance. San Francisco, CA: Jossey-Bass, 2009

2. Werner H. Erhard, Michael C. Jensen, Steve Zaffron and Kari L. Granger: Course Materials for: "Being a Leader and the Effective Exercise of Leadership – An Ontological/Phenomenological Model. Taught in Whistler, B.C., Canada, April 24, 2013

Chapter Eleven:

1. Howard Morgan, Phil Harkins and Marshall Goldsmith: The Art and Practice of Leadership Coaching. Hoboken, NJ: John Wiley and Sons, Inc., 2005

2. J. Robert Clinton: The Making of a Leader. Colorado, CO.: NavPress, 1988

3. Ibid.

4. Howard Morgan, Phil Harkins and Marshall Goldsmith: The Art and Practice of Leadership Coaching. Hoboken, NJ: John Wiley and Sons, Inc., 2005

5. J. Robert Clinton: The Making of a Leader. Colorado, CO.: NavPress, 1988

6. Howard Morgan, Phil Harkins and Marshall Goldsmith: The Art and Practice of Leadership Coaching. Hoboken, NJ: John Wiley and Sons, Inc., 2005

7. Ibid.

8. Dr. Myles Munroe: Passing It On: New York, NY: Faith Words, 2011

9. Ibid.

Chapter Twelve:

1. Stephen R. Covey: Principled Centered Leadership. New York, NY: Free Press, 1990

2. Ibid.

Chapter Thirteen:

1. Dr. Myles Munroe: The Spirit of Leadership. New Kensington, PA: Whitaker House Publishers, 2005

2. Ibid.

3. Ibid.

4. Ibid.

Chapter Fourteen:

1. Carmine Gallo: Five Reasons Why Optimists Make Better Leaders. Forbes Magazine. August 2012

Chapter Fifteen:

1. Stanley K. Ridgley: Strategic Thinking Skills. Chantilly, VA: The Great Courses, 2012
2. Ibid.
3. Steven Key: Five Reasons Projects Fail. Entrepreneur Magazine. September 2014
4. Jason Womack: Four Questions to Get the Project Going. Entrepreneur Magazine. May 2016

Chapter Sixteen:

1. John Jones, Deanne Aguirre and Matthew Calderone: Ten Principles of Change Management. Strategy+Business. April 2004

References

Chopra, Deepak, 2010. The Soul of Leadership. Harmony Books.

Clinton, J. Robert, 1988. The Making of a Leader. NavPress.

Covey, Stephen R., 1990. Principled Centered Leadership. Free Press.

DiMaggio, Joe, 2011. Conversations That Matter/Insights and Distinctions. Landmark Essays, Volume 1.

Gardner, Howard, 1993. Multiple Intelligences. Basic Books.

Gardner, Howard, 1995. Leading Minds. Basic Books.

George, Bill, 2004. Authentic Leadership. Jossey-Bass Publishers.

Giles, James, 1994. Essence of Greatness. Four Kings Publishers.

Goleman, Daniel, 1995. Emotional Intelligence. Bantam Books.

Jacobson, Ralph, 2013. Getting Unstuck: Using Leadership Paradox to Execute Confidence. Productivity Press.

Kouzes James M., and Posners Barry Z, 2008. The Leadership Challenge. Jossey-Bass Publishers.

Marquet, L. David, 2013. Turning The Ship Around. Portfolio Publishing.

Marshall, Tom, 1991. Understanding Leadership. Baker Book House Company.

Maxwell, John, 1995. Developing the Leaders Around You. Thomas Nelson Publishing.

McArthur, Bruce, 1993. Your Life: Why it is the way it is and what you can do about it. A.R.E. Press.

Morgan, Howard, Harkins Phil and Goldsmith Marshall, 2005. The Art and Practice of Leadership Coaching. John Wiley and Sons, Incorporated.

Munroe, Dr. Myles, 2005. The Spirit of Leadership. Whitaker House Publishers.

Munroe, Dr. Myles, 2011. Passing It On. Faith Words.

Raiport, Grigori, 1988. Red Gold. Tarcher Publishers.

Ridgley, Stanley, 2012. Strategic Thinking Skills. The Great Courses.

Seligman, Martin E.P., 2006. Learned Optimism. Vintage Publishers.

Strong's Concordance. 2010. Thomas Nelson Publishing.

Zaffron, Steve and Logan, Dave, 2009. The Three Laws of Performance. Jossey-Bass Publishers.

ABOUT THE AUTHOR: TONY MORRIS

Tony Morris Consulting

Leadership Training and Development

Contact Information:

Website: tonymorris.online

Facebook/Tony Morris

Twitter: iamtonymorris

About the Tony:

- International Leadership Consultant
- Workshop/Seminar Presenter
- Motivational/Inspirational Speaker

International Leadership experiences include:

Over the course of his career in personal, community and organizational leadership, Tony has gained a wealth of experience successfully managing teams, growing organizations and small businesses. He has a strong track record for directing strategic planning initiatives, developing marketing strategies, increasing community involvement and building highly productive leadership teams. He has initiated or supported the starting of six different successful organizations.

International Consulting Services include:

- Design and develop leadership programs and individualized curricula

- Analyze leadership program needs

- Evaluate small businesses and organizations for leadership reviews

- Provide classroom and seminar instruction and staff development workshops

- Conduct leadership development training and strategic planning workshops

Inspirational and Motivational Speaking

- Conduct seminars, workshops and retreats for the public and private sector of small business, and community organizations.

ABOUT THE CO-AUTHOR: JON JAMES

Jon James is the founder of Ignited Results, a full service digital inbound marketing firm where he creates automated customer attracting systems for his clients. The firm specializes in Search Engine Optimization (SEO), reputation management and leveraging conversion funnels to help automate client-acquisition campaigns for its clients.

As a serial entrepreneur, Jon has successfully built many companies over the last 20 years and is currently the founder of the new niche search engine BlackResults.com. Jon utilizes the search engine as leverage to test various online marketing strategies and SEO techniques which he then implements on behalf of his digital marketing and coaching clients.

He often sees the sunrise after an hour and a half of meditation and frequently utilizes that time of stillness to see his client's projects functioning profitably at their highest purpose and maximum outcome.

BOOKS BY TONY MORRIS

ORDER YOUR COPY AT
tonymorris.online

www.ingramcontent.com/pod-product-compliance
Lightning Source LLC
Chambersburg PA
CBHW062202280526
45788CB00001B/412